SpringerBriefs in Sociology

SpringerBriefs in Sociology are concise summaries of cutting-edge research and practical applications across the field of sociology. These compact monographs are refereed by and under the editorial supervision of scholars in Sociology or cognate fields. Volumes are 50 to 125 pages (approximately 20,000- 70,000 words), with a clear focus. The series covers a range of content from professional to academic such as snapshots of hot and/or emerging topics, in-depth case studies, and timely reports of state-of-the art analytical techniques. The scope of the series spans the entire field of Sociology, with a view to significantly advance research. The character of the series is international and multi-disciplinary and will include research areas such as: health, medical, intervention studies, cross-cultural studies, race/class/gender, children, youth, education, work and organizational issues, relationships, religion, ageing, violence, inequality, critical theory, culture, political sociology, social psychology, and so on. Volumes in the series may analyze past, present and/or future trends, as well as their determinants and consequences. Both solicited and unsolicited manuscripts are considered for publication in this series. SpringerBriefs in Sociology will be of interest to a wide range of individuals, including sociologists, psychologists, economists, philosophers, health researchers, as well as practitioners across the social sciences. Briefs will be published as part of Springer's eBook collection, with millions of users worldwide. In addition, Briefs will be available for individual print and electronic purchase. Briefs are characterized by fast, global electronic dissemination, standard publishing contracts, easy-to-use manuscript preparation and formatting guidelines, and expedited production schedules. We aim for publication 8-12 weeks after acceptance.

More information about this series at http://www.springer.com/series/10410

Pedro Paulo Gomes Pereira

Queer in the Tropics

Gender and Sexuality in the Global South

Forewords by Richard Miskolci and Judith Butler

 Springer

Pedro Paulo Gomes Pereira
Department of Preventive Medicine
Federal University of Sao Paulo (Unifesp)
São Paulo, São Paulo, Brazil

ISSN 2212-6368   ISSN 2212-6376   (electronic)
SpringerBriefs in Sociology
ISBN 978-3-030-15073-0   ISBN 978-3-030-15074-7   (eBook)
https://doi.org/10.1007/978-3-030-15074-7

Library of Congress Control Number: 2019934421

This Springer imprint is published by the registered company Springer Nature Switzerland AG
The registered company address is: Gewerbestrasse 11, 6330 Cham, Switzerland

For Maria Tereza (in memoriam),
Bárbara, and Daniela

You are quite aware: we want to pass a river swimming, and pass; but it's going to lead to the other side to a point a lot further down, quite different from what was expected.
Guimarães Rosa, Grande Sertão Veredas
(The Devil to Pay in the Backlands)

Foreword by Richard Miskolci

Queer in the Tropics is a book about experiences of abjection and of subjective resistance far from Europe and the United States. During past centuries of colonization, Europeans imagined that lands without sin or guilt lay under the equator. This mythos projected the tropics to be a perfect terrain for utopias but also for dystopias, a paradise with pleasure and life but also a potential hell full of violence and death. The tropics were a kind of distorted double of civilization, of the Global North, Europe or the United States. As heir to this imaginary, Pedro Paulo Gomes Pereira's work shows how we from the Global South see the world through our historical, political, and cultural relations to the dreams and nightmares of the North.

From here, we look at the world not only as marked by the material experiences of colonization, exploitation, and economic and political dependence on the Global North but also through the lenses of those marked by the cultural experience of being categorized as exotic and as intellectually inferior. Despite our advances in international scientific fields throughout the last half-century, most of our academic production is rarely recognized beyond Latin America. Our colleagues from the Global North may eventually read translations of our work, but they still do not quote us in their texts and books; in other words, they do not recognize us as their interlocutors.

This is especially unfair in the field of queer studies, where scholars ought to be more attentive to and critical in regard to processes of normalization like those that maintain the political economy of knowledge in which the United States and Europe become the incarnation of the world's brain and in which the tropics have been relegated to be – as the old adage states – "the asshole of the world" [*"o cu do mundo"*] (Pelúcio 2014, p.31). Thus, queer theory – so critical when regarding inequalities within national borders – maintains thought from the Global South in an abject relation to (or dependence on?) the North, thereby overlooking its own responsibility in international intellectual exchanges (Miskolci 2014).

After all, even those voices heard in the Global North regarding these kinds of inequalities tend to be those of immigrants who write about the tropics from within the Global North. With all due respect to our colleagues in this intellectual geopolitical battle, researching and writing from the tropics are not the same as doing so from within the old colonial powers. *Queer in the Tropics* proves this point through Pereira's concise reflections regarding some of the main issues around which queer knowledge has developed.

Among other characteristics that this book holds in common with most research conducted in Latin America is its empirical base. Historically, Brazilian social sciences and related disciplines have a tradition of linking theoretical reflection to empirical work. In anthropology and sociology, fieldwork tends to be carried out ethnographically. Therefore, our queer theory emerges through observation and analysis of the lived experiences of embodied subjects. Compared to the production of queer theory in the United States and Europe – which tends to be theoretical and developed through philosophy, literature, and cultural studies – Brazilian queer studies began and developed in relation to praxis.

From Néstor Perlongher's classical ethnography of male hustlers in the 1980s to the emergence of queer scholars such as Berenice Bento, Pedro Paulo Gomes Pereira, and Larissa Pelúcio in the early 2000s, common intellectual ground has paved the way for a creative segment of queer studies in Brazil. In constant and critical dialogue with the queer production from the United States, a group of diverse intellectuals, such as Guacira Lopes Louro, Karla Bessa, and others, have created our tradition of research in the field even when working from a historical perspective.

Here in the tropics, Pereira explores how experiences of abjection develop in a local way that cannot be understood simply by adopting concepts and theories created within the realities of the United States or Europe. *Queer in the Tropics* is simultaneously an ethnographic work and a theoretical reflection on how to create dialogue with queer theory from the Global North, instead of merely adopting it as a model to be applied elsewhere. The impulse behind Pereira's endeavor is not of theoretical xenophobia but rather a commitment to the spirit that unifies what he understands to be queer everywhere: a critical knowledge of the role of gender and sexuality in social relations.

The current political economy of knowledge is established upon unequal intellectual exchanges that prioritize knowledge produced in the Global North, especially in the United States. *Queer in the Tropics* shows that this unfair exchange not only updates old colonial relations shaping current scientific networks but also creates an acritical disciplinary framework that domesticates knowledge. Pereira's reflections cannot be reduced to a queer version of postcolonial or decolonial thought nor a sort of Brazilian queer of color critique. His objective is different, and it has the potential to enrich segments of critical thought to a wider discussion that have been obscured during their insertion into the English-speaking academic world.

Queer in the Tropics is a queer work in the sense that it is committed to the critical spirit that unifies queer studies from diverse origins. Thus, it is as queer as any other book written by an American or European scholar. But to be queer in a critical way, and to be based in the Global South, also implies preserving one's local origins and remaining coherent in relation to local aspects of the subjects who made this work possible. These subjects' affections and embodiments test the limits of queer theories from the Global North and the concepts that provincialize them. As such,

Queer in the Tropics is an original contribution that improves and enlarges queer studies through critical and truly global knowledge.

This ambitious contribution is made possible because of the book's vantage point. We in the tropics are removed from the center, contained within a relative marginality that allows researchers to absorb different intellectual traditions and to mix them. Outside of the United States and Europe, scholars are forced to incorporate other scientific productions while still creating their own. A relative marginality in relation to the center can be transformed into a richer perspective than the one circumscribed to a single intellectual context. As Brazilian essayist Oswald de Andrade proposed in his *Anthropophagic Manifesto* (1929/2017): we can choose to feed ourselves with the best of others so as to make our own work.

The adoption of the word *queer* to label our production here in the Global South can be interpreted as part of this cannibalistic means of feeding ourselves with the best of the center, incorporating it as part of ourselves so as to enter into a larger world of exchanges. From the beginning, our queer studies have been transnational and marked by critical perspectives in relation to normalizing processes that local LGBT studies did not dare to address. The focus on normalization and social control in the sphere of gender and sexuality fractured gay and lesbian studies as well as the queer segment that emerged from works like Pereira's (2004) early research into a therapeutic community for AIDS patients in Brasília.

How can a book that addresses the way in which Brazilian subjects deal with abjection attract the attention of and communicate to an English-speaking audience already testing the limits of what is recognized as queer theory? First, because it deals with a starting point that is common to much of queer studies: abjection. Second, because it does so in an original way, by establishing a new and critical dialogue with queer theory and its sources. Pereira invites his readers to see what it means to be queer in the tropics and how this cannot be fully recognized and understood simply by adopting previous theoretical and conceptual frameworks.

Tropically queer, Pereira introduces us to experiences of people who defy conceptions of normality and to queer theories available to understand such conceptions. In one of the chapters, we are introduced to Cida. Assigned male at birth in a poor central area of Brazil, Cida used hormones and body techniques to transform her body and become a *travesti*. Later, she moved to Europe, where she learned new languages and had access to other, different cultures. Eventually, she began abusing drugs and subsequently became HIV-positive. Back in Brazil, Cida deals with her HIV-positive status by combining medical treatments with frequent attendance at *Umbanda* rituals. Pereira contrasts Cida's life experience with that lived by Paul B. Preciado in order to think beyond Euro-American conceptions of the body, subjectivity, and the use of substances and body techniques.

In Pereira's reflection on the reactions against Judith Butler's visit to Brazil in 2017, he presents us with experiences proving that not all religious people are conservative, and that not all religions necessarily position themselves against queer people. Inclusive churches exist within Evangelical movements, and Afro-Brazilian religions often have an open approach to gender and to sexual fluidity. Avoiding any mechanical opposition between religion and progressive sexual politics, Pereira proposes considering how Butler could incorporate – both theoretically and liter-ally – an Afro-Brazilian religious experience and how that could affect and enrich her already precious work.

Queer in the Tropics guides us through diverse subjective and bodily experiences as a way of learning all along a given trajectory instead of at the end of the journey. As in Pereira's previous book, *De corpos e travessias* (*Of Bodies and Crossings* 2014), we are invited toward and attracted by the wanderings of his interlocutors, subjects who discover queer ways of dealing with power and inventing resistances. As in his reflection on life and biopolitics in the first chapter, we learn about differ-ent ways of understanding and resisting the relation between those allowed to live in a "normal" way and those relegated to the margins of social rejection.

In the tropics, Pereira's ethnographic work enters into dialogue – both respect-fully and critically – with queer theory and other intellectual sources from the Global North. He creates a rich and unexpected conversation that otherwise could not be possible, thus making the tropics a vantage point that travels back to the Global North in order to decolonize intellectual exchanges and propose future exchanges that might be of mutual recognition between the West and what it once considered the Rest.

Queer in the Tropics is part of this movement that attempts to turn the Western monologue into a dialogue with its twin Other. If the tropics were once a source of dreams and nightmares about the West itself, now the tropics want to dislocate the West from its old relation to alterity to a new one based on the recognition of the differences that bind us.

São Paulo, São Paulo, Brazil   Richard Miskolci

References

Andrade, O. (2017). *Manifesto Antropófogo*. São Paulo: Penguin/Cia das Letras. (Original pub-lished 1929).
Miskolci, R. (2014). Queering the geopolitics of knowledge. In S. E. Lewis, R. Borba, B. F. Fabrício, & D. de Souza Pinto (Eds.), *South-North dialogues on queer epistemologies, embodi-ment and activisms* (pp. 13–30). Bern: Peter Lang.
Pelúcio, L. (2014). Possible appropriations and necessary provocations a Teoria Cu. In S. E. Lewis, R. Borba, B. F. Fabrício, & D. de Souza Pinto (Eds.), *South-North dialogues on queer episte-mologies, embodiment and activisms* (pp. 31–52). Bern: Peter Lang.
Pereira, P. P. G. (2014). *De corpos e travessias: uma antropologia dos afetos*. São Paulo: Annablume.
Pereira, P. P. G. (2004). *O Terror e a dádiva*. Goiânia: Cânone Editorial.
Perlongher, N. O. (2008). *O negócio do michê: a prostituição viril em São Paulo*. São Paulo: Fundação Perseu Abramo.

Foreword by Judith Butler – Experiencing Other Concepts

Queer in the Tropics is a beautiful and demanding book by Pedro Paulo Gomes Pereira. It takes its reader into the life and death struggles of those who, excluded and shamed by a healthcare system, must navigate their own health and embodied existence, securing the conditions for their own lives. As a book, it stages a set of transformative contacts. In one sense, this book is an ethnography of travestis who struggle with healthcare issues – and institutions – with different interpretive frameworks. In the central chapters, the study turns to travestis who find in African diasporic religions vocabularies, images, and modes of interpretation that help them find their way through healthcare systems, legal vocabularies, medical treatments, and modes of healing and repair. Often, they develop within their own language an understanding of HIV, their own bodies as sites of desire and affliction, modes of persistence linked to communities of belonging, and a subtle practice of subversion in relation to institutions from which they are excluded. In another sense, this book is much more than an ethnography. It is a rhythmic movement between narrative and reflection; it starts and stops in the course of a set of encounters in which the theory-minded ethnographer cedes control, succumbs to grief, considers flight, but continues the accompaniment. In effect, this book asks us to stay with questions of life and death even when the difficulties of understanding demand translation, demand that we become something other than what we took ourselves to be. What happens in this book is rich description, but it not merely descriptive. It is the halting story of intense relationships, of mutual transformation, of cultural translation, and of collective practices of producing a new map of the possible.

Pereira's work moves between narrating the stories of the lives of travestis, understanding the conventions and norms of African diasporic religions that they pass on to one another, reflecting their relationships in their sorrow and persistence. At once a registry of affects and a theoretical investigation, the text never decides the essential or unitary meaning of *travestis* life. Rather, it records, and reflects upon, the various relations to others, to institutions, and to technologies in which those lives are crafted and reproduced in temporally saturated situations. Indeed, in this account, a travesti's life is neither simply "performed" nor is it the result of an engagement with technologies in the broadest term. It is rather the embodied form of relationships within which both performance and technology operate. In this way, Pereira offers a sympathetic but critical rejoinder to Paul Preciado's account of the technological production of gender, underscoring the relational life-worlds and the institutions and practices by which they are constituted and which, for the sake of their own lives, they must sometimes oppose. At the same time, this text engages theoretical work on the body, including the important work on queer theory emerging from Brazil (including the trenchant work of Richard Miskolci, Larissa Pelúcio, and Berenice Bento, among others), queer and decolonial theory (and their intersection), the sociological theory of Pierre Bourdieu, the anthropology of Eduardo Viveiros de Castro, and the European theoretical work of Foucault, Esposito, and Agamben. All of these theories can be brought to bear on the life of travestis, the biopolitical predicament and the status of their social practices, but none of them suffices as a definitive framework. They can, however, only touch upon these lives, or foreground questions about how to think about embodiment, technology, transmitted cultural traditions, power, violence, sexuality, the imaginary, desire, and hope. As theory, they have to be translated into another language, another set of concepts and lived experiences, and re-translated and re-worked from within a world excluded from their imaginings.

Pereira writes: "the construction of *travestis'* bodies does not depend only on hormones, silicone, or biomedical and corporal techniques; it is based on the relationships between people and spiritual entities. These relationships take place among families, among neighbors, and in religious settings. They take place among travestis and between *travestis* and *caboclos, pomba-giras, bombadeiras*, hormones, and silicon, all acting together in inventing bodies." This process of "invention of the body" can start before one is born, he tells us, when, for instance, spirits bring a body into existence, that safeguard that existence, are part of its formation, part of who the embodied being comes to be.

Pereira considers in detail a travesti's life as it exists within communities constituted within the terms of African diasporic religions. One crucial dimension of a travesti's life in Candomblé and Umbanda is how to interact with medical institutions that conceive illness and problems related to sexuality and desire in very different terms. For instance, Pereira tells us that often travestis have a *Pomba Gira*, the spirit of a former sex worker known for the schemes she has developed to dominate men. As a spirit, she is embodied by the travestis, helps to bring about womanhood, and remains an incorporated feature of that gender. This process of incorporation is complex. One is touched and transformed by the spirit, and the spirit becomes part of the very formation and accomplishment of gender itself. That otherness remains, but it is an internal alterity. The self is no longer enclosed on itself, but rather defined by its openness to alterity and the transformations that take place as a result of that opening. But even this theoretical formulation abstracts from the practice and process and can only be the result of a partial and inadequate translation. Indeed, every practice of incorporating a spirit involves a translation from one being to another, one facilitated by contact of some kind. The vast contribution to gender theory accomplished by Pereira's text thus has everything to do with the relation between translation and incorporation. For it is not only that a spirit, another body, a practice, an institution, and a technology touches the body or enters into its life processes, but that this alterity is itself a transformed and transformative feature of who one is. No one invents a gender identity on his or her own or as a result of an individual will. On the contrary, it is from this complex process that gender is instituted and transformed as a dynamic and complex process, and it is only within the terms of this dynamic complexity that one can begin to understand the sense in which gender is an "invention.".

"Invention" is central to Pereira's complex and persuasive study – a practice of invention itself. In some ways, the text is an extended meditation on the meaning of "incorporation": what spirits, substances, institutions, and worlds do we take into the body, and how are they – and we – transformed in the course of that incorporation? His theory does not proliferate new categories or seek to define all travestis in one way. It does, however, underscore the inventive effects of forms of contact that change all the surfaces and depths in the scene, whether that contact is with spirits or technology, imagery, or institutions.

Pereira is well-known for asking what form queer theory now takes in the Global South. Drawing on queer of color research, feminist theory (Rita Segato), and decolonial theory (Mignolo), he tracks the forms that queer theory takes in Latin America once it is unanchored from the urban centers of the Global North and European narratives of modernity. For Pereira, queer theory in Brazil and throughout Latin America has to undertake a decolonial turn. He does not refuse all theory from the North, but he makes distinctive use of a range of theories, many of which are formally incompatible with one another. This theoretical syncretism is itself part of the inventive practice that he theorizes. He makes use of what is important to think about this question; at the same time, he remains free of the orthodox version of every theory. But what changes in that theory once it comes into contact with Candomblé? With travestis life and its imaginaries? With the biopolitics of hormones and silicone, with religion, and with healthcare in the Latin American context? Throughout this text, he underscores the agency that travestis construct within African diasporic communities in Brazil, making use of their exclusion from dominant frameworks to fathom another horizon of possibility. Toward the end of his remarkable book, Pereira offers the following imagining: "perhaps the path forward is to enchant ourselves with the multiplicity of agents and their inaudible forms of agency, with the creativity of their poetics: tearing apart this reifying machine; avoiding the emulation of movements that wind up imprisoning us all; experiencing other concepts; and experiencing ourselves through other concepts." He gives me more credit than I desire for the originality of his own thought, but I affirm his company as interlocutor, as someone whose thought touches my own, who transforms those who take his words in, and who are enabled to think possibility in new and vibrant ways. In the end, if we are lucky, we are accompanied by one another, and who we are is not quite thinkable apart from that company.

Berkeley, California, EUA   Judith Butler

Contents

Chapter 1
Introduction

At the end of the 1990s, I was in the process of completing more than 2 years of fieldwork at an NGO on the urban periphery of Brasília for people living with AIDS. The institution housed patients affected by the epidemic, mostly people who had gotten sick and who, after a period of hospitalization, did not have anywhere to go or to care for themselves, as well as prisoners who had suffered without any assistance or treatment, and homeless people with no means of supporting themselves. The NGO functioned on an exclusively charitable basis, without any intervention or support from Brazil's government. It cared for all kinds of people, a landscape of members of the urban poor, excluded and rejected people, and people living precariously, conditions that originated in the close relations between the AIDS epidemic, social abandonment, and Brazil's extreme socioeconomic inequality (Pereira 2004; 2014).

While I was carrying out my fieldwork, Brazil's Federal Government released data showing a 50% reduction in deaths and an 80% reduction of opportunistic infections thanks to the use of anti-AIDS drug cocktails. At this time, the Federal Government made 15 antiretroviral medications freely and universally available. These advances in the fight against AIDS cannot be removed from the context of the Brazilian public healthcare system.

In 1988, Brazil's new federal constitution took effect, creating the Unified Health System [Sistema Público de Saúde (SUS)], the country's public healthcare system. Unified Health System offered all of Brazil's citizens complete, universal, and free access to healthcare. Widely regarded as one of the world's best public healthcare systems, Unified Health System attends to nearly 190 million people. Treatment of HIV/AIDS in Brazil is regarded as every citizen's right, supported by an effective articulation between different sectors of government and civil society. Unified Health System was inaugurated in 1988, the same year in which December 1 came to be defined as World AIDS Day, and that Brazil created the First Center for Serological Orientation and Support (now known as the Center for Testing and Counseling). Brazil's public healthcare system and the AIDS epidemic are contemporaneous, and both arise in the context of the country's re-democratization. The fight for a universal public healthcare system that aims to guarantee complete, universal, and egalitarian access to Brazil's population and the fight against the AIDS epidemic are both contemporaneous with struggles for democracy.

However, if public policies targeting the epidemic made a reduction in mortality possible throughout Brazil and proved to be successful in many aspects, medical and hospital-based dispositives did not appear to be especially effective for extremely poor populations (see, for example, Biehl 2007; 2011). At least within the individual realities of patients at the institution where I conducted my research, the Brazilian public healthcare system's actions against AIDS either did not arrive or were not effective. One of the reasons for this, as I learned over the course of my investigations, is that antiretroviral therapy does not only depend exclusively on medications, but also on actions and technologies aimed at effective adherence to drug regimens. First and foremost, this therapy cannot progress when confronted with a situation in which social and economic rights are absent. In addition, during a long period of time, the operation of "AIDS dispositives" (Perlongher 1987) increased the distance between healthcare services and dissident bodies; in point of fact, this sort of operation continues to this day. The AIDS epidemic in Brazil reinforced the heterosexual norms that served to pathologize dissident bodies. Within the initial discourse of "at-risk groups," the "AIDS dispositives" acted to control and normalize affective and sexual relationships in accordance with heteronormative patterns (Pelúcio and Miskolci 2009).

Patients at the NGO where I carried out my ethnography included former inmates, sex workers, children who lived on the street, intravenous drug users, alcoholics, and a significant number of sexual minorities such as gay men, lesbians, *travestis,*[1] and bisexuals, all confronting the HIV/AIDS epidemic. Here, bodies and subjectivities placed themselves apart from discourses of prevention and from the norms and directives for the treatment of AIDS patients; indeed, they placed themselves at a distance from the Unified Health System itself. Over the course of my investigations, for example, I registered the difficulties that *travestis* encounter in accessing the healthcare system; this problem persists and constitutes one of the major challenges facing Unified Health System. Here, I understand "access" as including a physical place of refuge for patients in need, as well as the paths that patients travel within the system in search of having their needs met. Health care providers' prejudices; their refusal to use patients' preferred, "social" names[2] when attending to them; an unfamiliarity with the particular necessities of *travestis,* as well as mistreatment, acts of violence, and miscomprehension make access to health

---

[1]A form of self-designation used by people assigned male at birth and who engage in different levels of corporal transformations so as to construct a more feminine form of corporal presentation, as seen below.

[2]Historically, legal name changes in Brazil have been extremely difficult. One workaround option for transgender people and others has been the use of "social names" which are preferred, but not legally recognized. In recent years, some Brazilian government agencies have issued identification documents with "social names"; additionally, legal name changes for transgender people have become, if not streamlined, at least easier to obtain. (T.N.)

services enormously difficult, if not impossible. Generally speaking, *travestis* do not utilize the healthcare system to treat depression, fever, or high blood pressure, but instead only when they are victims of violence and require first aid, or else when they seek out specific AIDS-related treatments. Even in these cases, however, they approach the system cautiously and with suspicion. Somehow, these bodies and subjectivities interpellate the "AIDS dispositive" and its moralizing grammars. By "interpellate", I mean to say that they demonstrate its limits and its inadequacies; they signal the need for other grammars that promote different forms of care.

Something within me changed after I began to interact with these interlocutors. Their intensity, their conformations, and their multiplicities seduced me. This experience moved me far more than I could have imagined. In trying to understand the AIDS epidemic without planning or controlling my own experiences – as I describe further in the chapter *Queer in the Tropics* – I came face-to-face with the stories and formulations of *travestis* through their performances and corporal reconstructions. With them, I learned that if societies invent forms of regulating and materializing sex for specific subjects – and if these "regulatory norms" demand to be repeated, cited, and reiterated constantly – twists and lapses in the process will still exist. These twists and lapses are most visible in the bodies that do not conform directly to the rules that regulate them, and that never adhere fully to the norms imposed on their materializations. As Butler (1990) writes, the invention of bodies presupposes their continuous reinvention. Here, it is worth emphasizing that I arrived at Judith Butler's work and at queer theory in general by thinking about the dissident bodies with which I had interacted, and about my experiences in the research that I conducted; bodies expressing their discomfort and their differences that could not be assimilated, and that stubbornly insisted on being *present*, signaling and constructing new possibilities in the world of the possible (as we will see, for example, in Chap. 4).

As I accompanied the dilemmas of Brazil's public healthcare system, I turned to investigating subjects such as the therapeutic itineraries of AIDS patients; adhesion to antiretroviral treatments; and the paths taken by *travestis* in the healthcare system. Over the course of time, I learned that one cannot stop a research project simply because one wants to: ethnographic experience is always within us. Experiences we live through during fieldwork can be recalled or reinterpreted years later, to be considered or conceived of in new ways (Peirano 2014; Matsue and Pereira 2017). Perhaps this is why – more than a decade after finishing my fieldwork – I returned to my experiences with the *travestis* I met in a housing shelter in Brasília's urban periphery. Revisiting field notes, interviews, and photographs to jar my memory, I reencountered figures who accompanied me over the course of my ethnographic work and found that only now could I truly manage to listen to something they had told me at the time. This, in turn, led me to the universe of Afro-Brazilian religions (Chaps. 2, 3, and 4).

I became enchanted with the poetics of the *travestis* with whom I had discussed corporalities and embodiments. I was impressed with their corporal constructions and with the ways they conducted their lives. First and foremost, I learned that they utilize certain philosophies derived from Afro-Brazilian religions in order to interpret both the world and their own corporal transformations. I should note, however, that in using this affirmation, I do not intend to reduce these religions to an intellectual and cognitive system, a risk to which Goldman (1990) alerts us. I became enchanted with the sophisticated forms of agency that *travestis* create in order to deal with the exclusionary actions of the power that establishes categories of what is permitted to enter into the world of the possible, codifying *travestis'* own bodies and subjectivities as unthinkable.

In this book, most episodes relating to Afro-Brazilian religions are from Santa Maria, a city in the state of Rio Grande do Sul. However, there are also experiences from my ethnography at an institution for AIDS patients in Brasília, as well as from research projects that I am currently conducting in downtown São Paulo. Brazil contains a vast panorama of Afro-Brazilian religions; every region of the country contains specificities and divisions of ritualistic modes of expression. Throughout the text, I have aimed to explain these differences and to define certain terms, always availing myself of the incredibly rich body of anthropological literature produced in Brasil. I am not an expert on this subject; rather, I arrived at it through interlocutors who allowed me to be affected by their experiences. Over the course of this process, I have learned that these bodies and subjectivities pull us out of ourselves to such an extent that this book is not *about* something or someone; instead, it is a registry of affections and affects.

***

The chapters that follow aim to rethink and engage with these enchantments and these affects. *Queer in the tropics* is an experience-book that registers attempts to respond to interpellations that have affected me. Though these experiences have produced a multiplicity of responses within me, they all articulate similar preoccupations: namely, bodies and their itineraries, and the trajectories of theories.

This is how, over the course of the book, AIDS patients appear, sometimes running away from institutions, or else wandering[3] or travelling through urban centers; other times, the narrative focuses on *travestis'* itineraries through *casas-de-santo*[4] and through the healthcare system. In the first chapter, I emphasize the significance of the terms my interlocutors use, such as: losing oneself, heading out, running away, escaping, and wandering/being errant. The expressions they use to describe these moments of errant movement are terms of dislocation and of movement. Reflecting on this semantic field could lead us to conclude that subjectivities are also located in that which exceeds and escapes norms; furthermore, under the influence of biopower operating on bodies and souls, something always dislocates, leaks out, and escapes. In this first chapter, based on an ethnographic study that I carried out mapping some of the principal approaches to biopower, I highlight tensions

---

[3] The Portuguese verb "errar" (to wander or to ramble) can also mean "to err" (a duel meaning that English maintains in the archaic sense of "errant"). In future usages, I have aimed to maintain something of this intentional ambiguity. T.N.

[4] The terms *saints' house* and *terreiro* designate the religious space of Afro-Brazilian religions. It is a space with its own distinct rituals, relationships, and social dynamics.

between politics that incentivize and aim to potentialize the lives and the existence of people who have been excluded and left to die, such as those that I met on the periphery of Brasília. This argument is based on two types of inquiries: the first examines the existence of biopolitical frameworks that simply produce bodies and subjectivities as fruits of circumscribed exercises of power and control, while the second asks how to read these kinds of narratives in the tropics. In the chapter, *On the Poetics of Incorporation,* I return to experiences of transit and flux, reflecting now on the processes of invention of *travestis'* bodies, by way of their stylistic economy, fabrication of beauty, and invention of complex forms of incorporation.

The movements of concepts exist within the flux of bodies and subjectivities. Over the course of reading, it will become clear that, here, there is no search for the exegeses of a singular author, much less the adoption of any single theory or theoretical framework. On the contrary, the text casts doubt on simply applied theories, as these cases *un-know* the fact that theories also travel and forget the unexpected nature of these encounters. When theories travel, they also dislocate, becoming something different: travel, transit, and itineraries affect them in shaking, distorting, and amplifying movements. Transits are often complicated and unequal. Much of what circulates as "universal theory" is rooted in experiences of Europe and the United States, which produce generic concepts that act in spaces where universal theory is tested and refined (Connell 2010). What I wish to emphasize here is that other-experiences produce something more, and that if the exercise of the "permanent decolonization of thought" (Viveiros de Castro 2009, p. 12) behooves us, we must also take up the task of understanding truncated flows and mistaken translations in the same movement with which we aim to expand and deepen cultural experiences. I am particularly interested in dislocation and transit, and in the meetings and encounters that they produce.

It is along these lines that, in the chapter *Queer in the Tropics,* I describe intricate itineraries of "strange" bodies. Encouraged by the experiences of transit of *queer* bodies in Brasil – and the interpellation of their own theories and inventions – I reflect on the possibility of the *queer* political' gesture opening itself to other-knowledges (e.g., opening itself to formulations of other-questions). I also reflect on the possibility that we might instead be imprisoned within a form of thinking that carries out an unmovable flow from the center to the periphery without our being able to propose or glimpse anything new. I seek to problematize both the potency of *queer* theory as well as its possible limits by formulating the following inquiries: are we faced with another theory that goes from the center to the peripheries (and that simply re-inscribes this center-periphery division in other colors)? How might we consider *queer* theory in the tropics or in the Global South? The term "tropics" aims to escape the idea of a geographically delimited nation or territory; here, it serves as a metaphor to designate the Global South. As Velho (2016) noted, we cannot forget that the South is not only a geographic concept, but also multiple trails that, historically, have already been "somewhat opened everywhere, and yet still remain in a subaltern positions" (Velho 2016, p.791).

Reflecting further on what *queer* is here in the tropics and attempting to accompany the complex and unforeseeable journeys of theories, I seek to delineate the principal contours of the meeting between *queer* theory and decolonial thought. This attempt aims to formulate questions such as: could the meeting of decolonial thinking and *queer* theory produce something more, so that we might speak – as enunciated in the title of the chapter – of "decolonial *queer*" thought? Or are these theories incompatible, inasmuch as the English-language *queer* signals toward a geopolitic that decolonial thinking aims to oppose? Do these proposals share anything in common? What is the potency of this meeting between theories, and what might it produce? And what movements might a *queer*, decolonial reading design? In attempting to bring myself closer to these lines of inquiry, *queer* theory and decolonial thought arise as open fields defining themselves exactly to the extent to which they affect and are affected by Others. What makes the meeting between these theories probable and fecund is that they are not modes of thought closed unto themselves, but rather movements of opening toward Others, of the insertion of other-theories and other forms of thinking and being.

Decolonial *queer* thought is a confluence to be constructed, as well as a confluence that we are constructing. Perhaps this is where its beauty and potential reside: in the movement of enchanting us with the multiplicity of our interlocutors and their unprecedented forms of agency, with the creativity of their poetics. The idea is to experiment with other concepts and to experience ourselves within other concepts. But decolonial *queer* thought is not the repetition, like an academic mantra, of a stock citation, an "in accordance with…", which might suggest a fixed theoretical framework to be applied (derived, for the most part, from the Global North). I will insist, in various moments throughout this book, that the most important consideration is that of the *bending* that we can affect. I also write of breaking with and recuperating theories, thereby producing something new (Chaps. 1, 3, and 5): I aim to *break with* the dispositive and the logic of coloniality; as well as using this effort to *alter* concepts, *transforming* them into forms that we might embrace differently and more fully. I refer to *bending* theories in the sense of twisting ourselves into spiral movements, but also in the sense of changing the direction of these theories. In other words, wrapping (or twisting) ourselves into these theories so as to give them new directions (Chap. 5).

Because this is a book about the travels of theories, dilemmas of translations arise in many different moments. It is not only a question of inquiring about the persistence of the English-language term *queer* in contexts like those of Brazil, but also of presenting the problem of how to work – in a book published in English – with terms that we use in Brazil. The contexts are different, and translations are oftentimes mistaken. We could consider here the difficulties of translating the term *travesti*: a form of self-designation used by people assigned male at birth and who engage in different levels of corporal transformations so as to construct a more feminine form of corporal presentation. There is a fluidity in the categories of trans* and *travesti* (Benedetti 2005), but *travestis'* conceptions of themselves – and the contrast they establish in relation to other categories, such as transexuality – suggest specificities in the formulation of gender that lead to my choice not to translate the expression *travesti*, in accordance with authors like Kulick (1998) and Pelúcio (2013). These translation dilemmas are also present in terms like mother- or father-of-a-saint[5]; saints' houses; *terreiro*, and so on. I have tried to approach these difficulties with translations, descriptions, footnotes, and references both bibliographical and filmic.

The astute reader will notice that I inquire about two dimensions: (1) The first consists in modulations of *agency*: can queer propositions of agency account for the forms chosen to express dissident bodies below the equator? Or, put another way: how do queer propositions of agency relate to chosen forms of expressing nonconforming bodies in the tropics? (2) The second dimension refers to dispositives that construct bodies and souls: are these dispositives universal? Do they act in the same way in all places and situations? Would the dispositives that construct bodies and souls act in similar ways in all places? And if the response is negative, what are the refractions that these bodies experience?

In order to answer these questions, I suggest, in a number of different movements throughout the book, that the issue is not simply a question of criticizing theories from the Global North or of formulating, here in the Global South, a default theory comprising already existent theories. The problem lies in taking these theories to be simply "applicable" to other realities that they do not produce, thereby decontextualizing them from their places of enunciation. And the great provocation is how to avail ourselves of their concepts while still subverting them based on shared and interwoven histories from our (post-) colonial context; in other words, seeing the colonial difference as an integral part of the theories elaborated here. This effort is directed toward altering concepts, transforming them so that they might contain more. This is a movement of breaking with the simple application of theories from the Global North, inverting and modifying their concepts and transforming them in such a way and with such intensity that they might produce something new, and so that they might speak more and speak differently. Furthermore, it is worth noting the corporeality of these theories, beyond the politics of localization and their places of enunciation.

The movement that I am proposing suggests the preeminent necessity of opening to other-theories: a propensity of queer theory in the tropics in its voyages, transversal journeys, and paths that pass through the experiences of bodies that transmit, trans-localize, and wander, and through sophisticated forms of agency. These bodies pass through other histories and sophisticated other-theories of sexuality and the body.

The book present figures who design other forms of agency and other manners of constructing bodies. For example, I show how, in Afro Brazilian religions – guided by the poetics of *travestis* with whom I converse about corporalities and embodiments –, these *travestis* construct sophisticated forms of agency to deal with their exclusion from the power that establishes categories of what can enter into the world of the possible, and that places their bodies and subjectivities as being

---

[5]A "father-of-a-saint" or "mother-of-a-saint" is the central authority figure within a casa de santo ou *terreiro*, responsible for leading both religious events and other activities. They express the will of the orixá who commands the terreiro. They are also called caretakers, because their task is to care for the saints, the *terreiro*, and for initiates (the children-of-a-saint).

unthinkable. I have also learned that philosophies exist that are rooted in the Afro Brazilian religions with which these *travestis* interpret the world and their own corporal transformations – although by making this affirmation, I do not intend to reduce these religions to an intellectual and cognitive system. These are theories that interest me more directly, and that are capable of bending theories from the Global North. I am truly proposing that my interlocutors elaborate theories. Presenting their visions and describing them densely is a way of presenting life-research and *transversal* political itineraries to the more interesting practices of queer theory and of contemporary social sciences and humanities.

In other words, this is a book of translations, of crossed readings, of conversations, and of inquiries. It is a book of conversations constructed over a period of time that remain unfinished and incomplete, signaling that the ideas that constitute them have yet to conclude. It may be that they cannot end; a book-experience is something unending – we must decide its final period. This is an arduous task for those who understand experiences as happenings (Beaulieu 2002), as instants of the spatial-temporal reception of affections and perceptions that – as Deleuze thought of bodies – are capable of making themselves into an infinite and intensive becoming.

***

One cannot weave a book like this alone. Every page was written in a constant process of learning and listening. I learned from Cida, with her sophisticated simplicity, and her attempts to teach me something of Afro-Brazilian religions; from Eduardo and his errant wanderings, his "bent" form of rambling through the city; the *travestis*, mothers- and fathers-of-saints, who did not hesitate to write to me so as to correct my affirmations, informing me that concepts I dealt with hastily were in fact quite dense. Others appeared on this same path: Martha Souza, a nurse who took me through the neighborhoods of Santa Maria, and Marcelo Niel, a psychiatrist and son-of-a-saint at Abassá de Babá, a *terreiro* of the Angola lineage, who recorded the beauty of the journeys of mothers-of-saints to New York. Both taught me a great deal, and I thank them immensely for their patience. José Jorge de Carvalho and his insistence on examining performances and the ritualistic character of religion; Otávio Velho, always showing, with his calm erudition, a blind spot in my analyses; Rita Segato, one of the Global South's greatest feminists; which I have the honor of having as a friend and eternal advisor Judith Butler, who read the book, inpired me with her critiques and gave me a wonderful preface; Gloria Careaga, who hosted me in Mexico and was a sensitive interlocutor; Guacira Louro, who, with her elegant writing and her sweet speech, is responsible for many of the good things that an entire generation has done and continues to do (the bad things are our responsibility). Richard Miskolci, Berenice Bento and Larissa Pelúcio are always present here, even when I have not cited them; in one way or another, they provoked everything I have written in this book. Richard not only read the texts but also corrected them with the keen eye of a friend and the rigor of an anonymous reviewer.

I would also like to thank my colleagues in my department at Unifesp, who gave me the time to carry out a post-doctoral fellowship that allowed me to finalize the book; the graduate program in sociology at the University of Brasilia, which hosted me and allowed me to conduct seminars and public discussions, in addition to seeing old friends; and Monica Schpun, from the Centre de Recherches sur le Brésil Colonial et Contemporain, École des Hautes Études en Sciences Sociales (CRBC/ EHESS), for hosting me in Paris with dense dialogues and unforgettable dinners. When I was finishing the book, I received support from FAPESP (Process nº 2019/17227-1, Fundação de Amparo à Pesquisa do Estado de São Paulo/ FAPESP).

The first chapter was translated by Philip Sidney Pacheco Badiz and the others by Raphi Soifer. At each step, Philip and, mainly, Raphi presented me with possibilities and limits, and attempted to take on translation dilemmas in such a way so as to preserve the tone and rhythm I conferred to the original Portuguese-language version. Edna, my friend and reviser, pulls my ear every once in a while, and always insists that I should "maintain my style." From her, I have learned that the form of writing is also a form of resistance.

Finally, as I have said, this is a book of experiences, of affections, and of affects.

References

Beaulieu, A. L'expérience deleuzienne du corps. (2002). *Revue Internationale de Philosophie, 4*(222), 511–522.

Benedetti, M. R. (2005). *Toda feita: o corpo e o gênero das travestis.* Rio de Janeiro: Garamond.

Biehl, J. (2007). *Will to live: AIDS therapies and the politics of survival.* Princeton: Princeton University Press.

Biehl, J. (2011). Antropologia no campo da saúde global. *Horizontes antropológicos, 17*(35), 227–256.

Butler, J. (1990). *Gender trouble: Feminism and the subversion of identity.* New York: Routledge.

Connell, R. (2010). *Southern theory: The global dynamics of knowledge in social science.* Cambridge: Polity Press.

Goldman, M. (1990). Candomblé. In: L. Landin, org., *Sinais dos Tempos: Diversidade Religiosa no Brasil.* Rio de Janeiro: ISER, 1, 123–130.

Kulick, D. (1998). *Travestis, sex, gender and culture, among Brazilian transgendered prostitutes.* Chicago: University of Chicago Press.

Matsue, R. Y., & Pereira, P. P. G. (2017). Quem se diferencia apanha (Deru kui ha watareru): experiência etnográfica, afeto e antropologia no Japão. *Mana, 23*(2), 427–454.

Peirano, M. (2014). Etnografia não é método. *Horizontes Antropológicos, 20*(42), 377–391.

Pelúcio, L. (2013). Illegitimate Pleasures: "tesão," eroticism and guilt in sex between clients and travestis in prostitution. In: H. S. S. Carrara et al., org., Sexuality, Culture and Politics: A South American Reader. Rio de Janeiro: CLAM, 490–507.

Pelúcio, L., & Miskolci, R. (2009). A prevenção do desvio: o dispositivo da aids e a repatologização das sexualidades dissidentes. In *Sexualidad, Salud y Sociedad: Revista Latinoamericana* (Vol. 1, pp. 125–157). Rio de Janeiro: CLAM-IMS-UERJ.

Pereira, P. P. G. (2004). *O terror e a dádiva.* Goiânia: Cânone.

Pereira, P. P. G. (2014). De corpos e travessias. In *Uma antropologia de corpos e afetos.* São Paulo: Annablume.

Perlongher, N. (1987). *O Que é Aids.* São Paulo: Brasiliense.

Velho, O. (2016). O que é pensar desde o Sul. *Sociologia & Antropologia, 6,* 781–795.

Viveiros de Castro, E. B. (2009). *Metaphysiques cannibales.* Paris: Presses Universitaires de France.

Chapter 2
In and Around Life

In the last chapter of *"La Volonté de Savoir"* (*The Will to Knowledge*) Foucault speaks about an era in which death no longer bludgeons life. The "threshold of biological modernity", he said, lies exactly where life enters history, ushering in "the era of biopower" (Foucault 1978, p. 140). Foucault describes modernity within the inseparability of biological life and political life – politics directed towards the government of life. Following the connotations conferred by Foucault, the concepts of biopower and biopolitics have become central in the social sciences and humanities; for some though, addressing them has become the most urgent challenge of contemporary thought.

Initially, I will seek to map some of the principal formulations of biopower and biopolitics, without attempting to be exhaustive, a position justified by the large number of commentators on the subject, including Fassin (2000, 2006a, b), Lazzarato (2000), Lemke (2011), Pelbart (2003). Then I will turn to two essential concerns: one that inquires about the existence of biopolitical frameworks that end up producing bodies and subjectivities as mere fruits of the exercise of power and control and, thus, are circumscribed by them; and the other that asks how we should read this scenario in the tropics. While contemplating these concerns, the text reflects on the possible limits and potentialities of this conceptual framework.

Make Live and Let Die

Michel Foucault outlined the main contours of the discussion concerning biopower and established a new way to theoretically explore the tension between make live and let die (Lemke 2011). Chronicling the unusual appearance of sex as a founder of identity and hence the intelligibility of the modern individual, Foucault (1978) argues that power, which once struggled to avoid death, begins to focus on the production, regulation and maintenance of life. A productive power emerged that

P. P. G. Pereira, *Queer in the Tropics*, SpringerBriefs in Sociology,
https://doi.org/10.1007/978-3-030-15074-7_2

simultaneously controlled and generated that which it regimented. Thus, the power of death related to sovereign power was concealed by the administration of bodies and by the calculative management of life. Mechanisms of power that would eventually be directed toward the body and life, involving everything that helps proliferate and strengthen the species. The concept of biopower marks the moment in which power begins to invest in life. This process occurs through an anatomo-politics of the human body (maximizing its strengths to integrate it into efficient systems) and a biopolitics of the population, focused on the species body. A body that is imbued with the mechanisms of life: birth, morbidity, mortality, longevity, among others (Foucault 2003, 2008).[1] The importance given to health, demographic and urban policies in the eighteenth century is the first step towards a biopolitical characterization that penetrates the social spheres, through a process of the "governmentalization" of life.[2] – a process that extends from pastoral power to its confession techniques; from the reasons of State, to the knowledges of the police. Thus, biopower is a relatively streamlined set of actions developed by authorities to intervene in the sphere of human vitality: birth, development, disease and death. Life, then, assumes strategic importance.

Notwithstanding this history of a modernity that moves away from death and that ruptures with the era of epidemics, Foucault still alerts us to the existence of death practices patrolling this very modernity. Everything occurs as if the proliferation of forms of control and the maintenance of life are simultaneous to the processes of exclusion, of the creation of abject others, and even of attempts to extirpate parts considered undesirable. Thus it is an ambiguous movement: a juncture in a life that must be protected at all costs, the invention of others that threaten life, and the emergence of lives that do not deserve to be lived. Therefore, we live in a time when there is overvaluation and protection of life, while at the same time there are areas where people are left to die. Thinking on a global scale, it is interesting to recall that together with the growth in health policies, mass vaccination, innovations in science that provide people with quality of life and health, over the last few decades, we have endured conflicts such as Rwanda, Yugoslavia, Liberia and Sudan. The 1990s have come to be known as the decade of large-scale violence, characterized by an

---

[1] In his book *Society Must Be Defended* (*Il Faut Défendre La Société*), in which he imagines a succession of knowledge-power regimes, Foucault (2003, p. 243) stated, "After the anatomo-politics of the human body, established in the course of the eighteenth century, we have, at the end of that century, the emergence of something that is no longer an anatomo-politics the human body, but what I would call a 'biopolitics' of the human race." For Foucault, the power that emerged was not directed at the individual body, but at the "total mass" affected by the processes of life (birth, death, illness). Biopolitics deals with the population as a political problem and addresses the biological processes of the man-species, seeking to secure over these not discipline, but regulation (Foucault 2003, pp. 239–264).

[2] Governmentality is the object of studying forms of government. Foucault intended to encompass several dimensions of the modes of governing: the set of institutions, processes, analyzes, calculations and tactics that permit the exercise of power over the population, the tendency to manage the predominance of this type of power; a process that leads from a legal and administrative status to a state of population control and security (Castro 2009, pp.188–193). Regarding the concept, see Dean (1999), Gordon (1991), Malette (2006), Rabinow (1999) and Rabinow and Dreyfus (1995).

excess of anger that produced a creativity of degradation and violation: bodies maimed and tortured, people burned and raped, women disembowelled, children mutilated, sexual humiliation of all types, as Appadurai (2009) warned us.

Biopolitics, thus, presents irreconcilable aspects: it either produces subjectivities or death; it either turns the subject into its own object or the objective, it is either life politics or politics concerning life (Esposito 2004). This "ineffability", as Esposito would have it, led theoreticians to diverse pathways, either signalling that nowadays the concept of biopower signifies its productive character, or highlighting that one of the principal characteristics of contemporary biopolitics is the production of the *homo sacer*. Perhaps it is this tension in and around life that proportions such distinct positions as those observed in the formulations of Agamben (2004a, b) and the criticisms of these formulated by Rabinow and Rose (2006).

The Concept of Biopower in Dispute

Agamben argues for a close relationship between the three figures he considers central: sovereign power, *homo sacer* and the state of exception. Sovereign power establishes the limits between life that deserves to be protected and that which can be killed; life enters the political game, sheltered and empowered, or simply exterminated. The sovereign is simultaneously both within and outside the legal system, since it has the capacity to establish the state of exception. *Homo sacer* – the individual who can be killed without this death constituting a crime or a sacrifice – emerges from the inversion of the sovereign figure. This relationship between sovereignty, the state of exception and *homo sacer* is the very foundation of the organization of bodies in the West.

The most striking feature of modern life, for Agamben, is that the state of exception is increasingly becoming the rule, making the line that delimits the border between life worth living – and that, therefore, should be protected and encouraged – and bare life, with no guarantees and exposed to death, tenuous and unstable. Unlike Foucault, Agamben affirms that biopolitics did not emerge with modernity, rather it is at least as old as sovereign exception, given that since then, biological life has been placed at the centre of its calculations. The modern State merely clarifies the link between power and bare life, since biopolitics has existed since humans separated themselves from the animals and since biological life extended to political life (Fassin 2006b). Agamben shows that the core of biopolitics is the distinction between *zoe*, the simple fact of life common to all living beings – biological life – and *bios*, a way of living inherent to an individual or group, in which humans segregate themselves from animals, often qualified as political life. The dualism between *zoe* and *bios* form the fundamental categorical pair of Western politics. A characteristic of modernity is the growing confusion between *zoe* and *bios*.

If Agamben defines the basis of the relationship between sovereign, *homo saber* and the capacity of the former to institute the state of exception, Rabinow and Rose (2006) argue that these are extraordinary times, and the fundamental characteristic for defining biopower cannot be determined in the present. Indeed, biopower in contemporary States specifies a relationship between the power to make live and let die; what distinguishes and defines it are "strategies to govern life". In an attempt to map these strategies, Rabinow and Rose highlight the following dimensions: the appearance of new modes of individualization and conceptions of autonomy associated with the right to health, life, liberty and the possession of forms of happiness (understood in bodily and vital terms), the emergence of new types of patient groups and individuals who define their citizenry in terms of their rights; the outbreak of new circuits of bioeconomy; large-scale capitalization of bioscience and a mobilization of its elements into new relationships of exchange, establishing constitutive connections between life, truth and value.

With these dimensions in mind, Rabinow and Rose (2006) define biopower as truth discourses concerning the vital nature of human beings; a set of authorities considered competent to speak that truth; strategies of intervention in collective existence in the name of life and health; modes of subjectivation, in which individuals act on themselves in the name of life or individual or collective health. Rabinow and Rose show us the emergence of biosocialities, new forms of subjectivation, or how science can potentialize life.

In a book on the "The Politics of Life Itself" Rose (2007) defines biopolitics as strategies specifically related to human vitality, morbidity and mortality; the ways in which authorities and interventions are established that are defined and legitimized as the most effective and appropriate. For Rose, biopolitics is currently related to the work of biotechnology laboratories in the creation of new phenomena (and pathologies), to the computational power of devices that link clinical histories with genomic sequences, to the marketing powers of pharmaceutical companies, to the regulatory strategies of research, bioethics, and drugs and food surveillance committees, and to the pursuit of profits involving all of these.[3]

Regardless of these differences, it should be emphasized that a reading of biopower focused only on the potentialities of science, which is not supplemented by other attentive readings of forms of governing life over bodies (Fassin 2000), can omit frameworks like those I came across in my ethnography. Moreover, there are many moments in which science is called to sustain that which is a biologically better life and how to make it more powerful – a process that makes one life more powerful, but that can be consubstantial with death for lives considered biologically worse (Foucault 2003). The complexity of the politicization of life and the tension between make live and let die can be accompanied by the quantity and variety of theoretical approaches, which range from, as Fassin (2006a, p.40) duly pointed out, the horizon of the laboratory and bioinformatics, clinical immunology and genetic sequencing, assisted reproduction and cancer therapy, studied by Löwy (1996), Napier (2003), Rabinow (1999) and Rapp (2000), to camps of refugees and deportees, to social protection and to welfare programs, as analyzed by Agamben (2004a), Agier (2002), Bauman (1998) and Malkki (1995).

---

[3] Rose (2007) closely examines two crucial dimensions of contemporary biopolitics: the biological molecularization of human phenomena, and the centrality of the idea of vitality.

Given this context, how do we perceive situations like those I studied? Is a definition of biopower that obscures moments in which parts considered abject are relegated to death even possible? Is there a way to elude the tension that I perceived in my ethnography which placed that which is the most modern form of prevention and maintenance of life next to people who perceived themselves as the "junk of the world" (Pereira 2003, 2004, 2008) and for whom health policies have no effect? How can we escape the antinomy that places life that is protected beside excluded lives that circulate around death?

Immunization Paradigm

The AIDS epidemic brought significant changes in social relations, in forms of perceiving social differences, in the conceptions of health and illness, making us understand how a virus can transform society. The fear of contagion and the millennial terror of epidemics have intensified. The concept of miasma provided the conditions for the interruption of exchanges, because the metaphor of contagion – which is a trope of circulation – revives aseptic ideals that seek the symbolic cutting of one individual from another in an attempt to avoid possible contamination. The psychic trauma arising from pestilence and epidemics, reactivated by AIDS, encountered the potentially guilty and intensified the need to avoid proximity with likely sources of infection. The operation of locating the contamination in the "other" accrues mainly from the quest to understand the epidemic and to identify the contaminators. The deviant behaviour of the "other" makes the contagion intelligible, providing safety and distance from which to confront the trauma of the AIDS pandemic (Pereira 2004).

Responses to the epidemic were diverse and it would be extremely simplistic to reduce a complex scenario of State policies, the emergence of laws and norms and the mobilization of civil society in the fight against AIDS to a manifestation of aseptic ideals or fear of contagion (Bastos 1999). However, there is no way to avoid these aspects, which are embedded in the wider context of biopolitical devices, especially in scenarios like that of Brazil.

AIDS has mainly victimized the disadvantaged sectors of Brazilian society. Structures of inequality and social oppression have been exploited to leave millions of people in situations of acute vulnerability. In Brasilia, for example, someone in this situation is referred to the shelter where I developed my research, which I will describe more fully in the next section. In my ethnography (Pereira 2004), I was able to narrate how the symbolic cut occasioned by the advent of AIDS and extreme poverty drove nearly two hundred people to a process of social asepsis that removes the impure and undesirable parts, making it possible to group the homeless and those who roamed hospital corridors, health services, prisons and other correctional facilities, in one institution.

The centrality of notions like contagion and immunization in understanding the AIDS epidemic in Brazil is what led me to the work of Esposito (1998, 2002, 2004), which continues to reflect on the "enigma of biopolitics".[4] According to the author, we live moments of immediate superposition between politics and *bios* that form a double movement: the politicization of life and the biologization of politics – a process that places life at the centre of the political game, but produces thanatopolitics. Esposito reminds us, for instance, that it was Foucault who asked the question, "Why does a political life threaten to translate into a death practice?". To try to answer this enigma, Esposito formulated the idea of the "immunization paradigm": a tendency to protect life from risks implicit in the relations between men and women, to the detriment of the extinction of community ties. To defend preemptively against contagion, a portion of evil is injected into the body that you want to protect.

The invasive circumstances of contagion entreat measures of immunization. This configuration forms a key device of modernity: there are risks that must be identified so that protection measures can be developed, such as immunization. Esposito argues that if immunization is common to all eras and societies, only modernity institutes it as structure, establishing the immunization paradigm as central. The immunization device operates on the assumption of confronting the existence of evil and ends, in this movement, by reproducing the very evil that it aims to prevent. In social immunization, life is guarded in a way that may even deny the possibility of its existence (Campbell 2006; Castiel 2010).

The nucleus of Esposito's proposal approximates, for example, that which I recorded in my ethnography: terror contemplated as the interruption of exchanges, the centrality of the fear of contagion in everyday life, the feeling of the impossibility of relationships, occasioned by a certain type of social asepsis, risk as a habitual language (Pereira 2004); and ultimately, the use of terms such as terror, fear, dread, misgiving as a language of affections to discourse on the impossibility of creating ties and the rupture of exchanges. The fear of contagion segregates, in various spheres, including in hospitals, and the segregation is constituted as terrifying. The differences between what I described and the formulations of the author of *Bios* are numerous; however, the main issue resides in the mode of perceiving biopolitics: while Esposito speaks of an immunization paradigm, i.e. some sort of universal claim, my aspiration was merely to register a grammar that related the interruption of exchanges to a language of affections. Furthermore, I endeavoured to understand what emerged from this tension between the absence of the State, on the one hand, and the medical-therapeutic actions for AIDS patients, on the other.

The theories mapped in this text formulated proposals that when solicited to focus on the reality I had tried to describe and analyse in previous works (Pereira 2003, 2004, 2008), produced a certain dissonance. This situation generated concerns on which I intend to dwell, albeit briefly, and with no intention of exhausting the issues: 1) the first concerns the idea of a biopower that is exercised over agents, inciting and controlling them in all spheres, i.e. the presupposition of power transcendently acting on overly standardized beings who are perceived homogeneously; 2)

---

[4] The journal *Diacritics* (2006, v.36, n.2), devoted a special issue to Esposito (2006) with articles that provide an overview of the Italian philosopher's work.

the second is related to notions of modernity that are inferred from the authors previously mentioned, as well as possible ways of reading, here in the tropics, this scenario of a time when death begins no longer to bludgeon life.

Wanderings

In 1998 and 1999, I conducted an ethnography in a shelter for AIDS patients in which ex-prisoners, ex-prostitutes, homeless people, transvestites, people abandoned or evicted from their homes, users of injected drugs and alcoholics lived in a situation of confinement. Throughout the fieldwork, I repeatedly heard the term "terror": the internees were referring to the life they led between the shelter that received them and the hospitals; even while discussing their illnesses, they repeatedly and insistently used the term and the semantic field that it evoked. The narratives of the internees consisted of enunciates that composed a picture of isolation, loneliness and lack of communication. I suggested in my ethnography (Pereira 2004) that terror presented itself to internees as a systematic form of the breaking of relationships of gifting: the impossibility of creating ties, due to the disruption of gifting situations, especially in people who needed these ties to survive, evoked a state of stupor. It was the extreme ruptures in these kinds of relationships that could be characterized as one of the most prominent faces of suffering and terror.

I examined the processes through which terror was inscribed on the bodies, and became aware of the consciousness of these internees, occluding the horizon of meaning around them. I sought to present the strategies and methods of discipline used by the authorities in the institution,[5] placing the focus of exposure on the description and analysis of the bodily manipulation of the internees, and on the examination of discourses in which the constant theme was the imminence of death. The internees presented no forms of resistance regarding the cure, and the medicine and health services produced a field of amplified suffering. This plot ultimately formed a space of suffering, in which everyone was inserted – patients, institution authorities and health professionals.

I also accompanied these internees in their itineraries around hospitals and health services, particularly at the University Hospital of Brasília (HUB). In the hospital environment, I came face to face with public policies directed towards the epidemic, which comprised knowledge of prevention practices, involved the etiology of the disease and drug therapies and culminated in the general dynamics of the epidemic. It was this experience that brought me closer to the structure and methods of the "fight against AIDS" in the country and made me aware of the history of this disease.

If along the Esplanade of Ministries, public policies against AIDS in Brazil were being planned, and if in the city centre, health professionals handled sophisticated

---

[5] I use the terms refuge, shelter and institution interchangeably because these are the expressions most commonly used by my interlocutors (Pereira 2004).

forms of management and drug distribution, on the outskirts, on a farmstead on the margins of a satellite town of Brasilia, lived people for whom the policies had no effect. They were individuals living with HIV whose disease received no follow-up and who survived without assistance or direct intervention from the State. The struggle for forms of protection against the epidemic, policies to prevent contamination, actions in favour of life, like those declared in hospitals and divulged by public policies, stumbled across people excluded and relegated to death.

This abandonment and the exclusion proceedings were perpetrated concomitantly with the actions of State, which formulated and orchestrated preventive practices, adherence to antiretroviral treatment and free medication distribution. The existence of a refuge like this demonstrates that there is a zone where public policy is unable to enter or simply has no effect. When faced with the incapacity of reasonable therapeutic practices for 'those people', a doctor once told me: "Since reality cannot be changed, it's about saving those who can be saved, or taking care of those who can be cared for". Efforts directed towards 'those people' were useless. Not that treatment was refused the internees of the shelter, indeed, they roamed the health services of the Federal District, but, it was known that "they don't adopt care practices or adhere to the treatments". Therefore, "nothing can be done". "They are there to die", pronounced many health professionals, using a phrase I heard endlessly for more than 2 years. Performatizing a tension between making live and letting die, prevention policies, medications and forms of management sat side by side with people for whom such measures and actions never arrived, left to fend for themselves in a shelter for AIDS patients.

As I mentioned above, one of the concerns refers to the design of biopolitical frameworks that involve all relationships and control everything. Such a view ends up preventing an approximation to the complexity of the lived experience itself. Thus, a homogenization of the variation in individuals occurs, a product of certain design strategies that are merely an exercise of power and control, and which ignore the complexity and historicity of the agents. At least that was what I learned from Eduardo, one of my interlocutors. I want to talk a bit about him, of how I found him in a shelter for AIDS patients and our unexpected meeting not long after my fieldwork ended.

Eduardo told me his story as an internee of the refuge where I did my fieldwork. He was a puny man of 35, with light-coloured eyes, who had travelled around Brazil, passing through several cities until he arrived at Brasilia. Born in Praia Grande, on the coast of the State of São Paulo, he was raised on the streets, in an unusual situation: he was kidnapped by his father when he was six. His father intended to use him to beg on the streets, because Eduardo was beautiful and had light-coloured eyes, features that facilitated this activity. Moreover, the father taught him petty theft. For 6 years he travelled around cities and only at the age of twelve did he return to live with his mother in São Paulo.

She put Eduardo in school and started to impose hygiene practices and rigid rules of behaviour. He, did not adapt, however, and returned to live on the streets when he was about 17 years-old. He told me once peremptorily, "That life was not for me". The mismatch caused constant running away, until he decided not to return. Eduardo described an itinerant life: moving from town to town, roaming the streets, "wandering erringly in the great big world of my God". And it was during this walking that he became infected with HIV; a contamination he attributed to roadside cabarets and the use of injected drugs. The contours of his life were described at the time as "vagrancy": as a perennial meandering, enveloped in excesses and errors.

The infirmity eventually weakened him. When I first met him, he was unable to walk, was half his normal weight, a condition aggravated by various opportunistic infections, including tuberculosis that he had contracted at the time. It was as the "junk of the world" that he introduced himself. "I'm the leftovers", he told me several times, underlining what seemed to be his definition: "human leftovers". In this same conversation, he insisted on telling me the dramatic story of his first night at the shelter that housed him: other internees eventually made him sleep outdoors, fearful of being contaminated with tuberculosis. He had often slept in the open, but to imagine that his illness and his ailing body would cause so much horror? "I am what the rejects reject", he concluded.

The story of Eduardo – much more complex than I could hope to describe here –narrates something about exclusion and about intimate relationships between contagion and isolation that enabled his life and practices of exchange (of bodies, fluids) to be transformed into the condition of segregation and distance. Trying to understand biopolitics today involves understanding what processes construct a shelter for AIDS patients like the one that I studied and that enable a story like Eduardo's. What does it mean to understand how a country that stands out in the fight against AIDS (public policy, technology, universal and free distribution of anti-retroviral drugs, spectacular international fights to break patents, among others) creates these abject others, who see themselves as the "junk of the world".

However, this is not the entire story of Eduardo. One year after the end of my fieldwork, I bumped into him at the door of the HUB. Although he was in a hurry, I asked him to talk with me. He wove brief remarks concerning the people I had met and with whom I had lived during my research and offered information concerning the progress of the institution that had housed him. That's when I realized that we were walking, away from the hospital, and already crossing the street, toward the blocks of the North Wing. There, an unusual itinerary began, that I had been unable, for various reasons, to follow until then. This itinerary allowed me to perceive dimensions that were unachievable in research focused on institutions (in the refuge or hospitals), like the one I had conducted.

That day, Eduardo walked the streets with resourceful assurance. He obtained money for his immediate needs: asking for money on the street, in bars, at the bakery, modifying his body posture accordingly. Immediately, he acquired a circumspect tone, returning to a peaceful countenance when speaking with me. He knew restaurateurs and, as time passed, he "hustled" two "takeaways", which were our lunch. He recognized the grammar of the city, walking fluidly in the "between-blocks" of Brasilia, inventing pathways. He wielded a vocabulary of slang with which he developed communication so rapidly and specifically that I got lost in their modulations. Eduardo told me about his love life. He said he had been in a relationship with a beautiful woman, but he could not manage "to be with one person only." "I'm a big slut," he said. In a few short minutes, he told me how he loved having sex with more than two people, as well as in public places, and that he had relations with men and women. Most of all, he liked variety. The only person who understood him was a *travesti* with whom he had maintained a relationship for several years, because she allowed him to be "more free." However, Eduardo eventually "ran away." In all, Eduardo taught me something about the transit of bodies and subjectivities with which I had come into contact over time, and that I only came to understand more densely some time after our walk through the city.

And so I spent the day walking through the North Wing, in a sense, cutting it diagonally. Whoever observed Eduardo on that walk, along that crooked itinerary, could see a "bare life", relegated to its own devices. But he, despite the penury, was more. Eduardo had found an *"in-between"* that my ethnography, I repeat, concentrated on institutions, could not follow. This invention of a possible precarious *in-between* allowed him to slip away, slide down, seep out. In these itineraries, Eduardo was not just the target of drug therapies, nor exclusively the object of a medical power that controlled everything, nor was he only the "junk of the world" dumped in a shelter for AIDS patients, nor only a denuded life exhibiting its precariousness and irrelevance in a social landscape already overly saturated, much less the simple product of an immunization system that wanted to prevent the contamination and pollution of abject beings. Perhaps, since he was all of this, he was *more*. A *more* that made him escape that day, conforming to my last image of him: walking the streets, wandering in his intricate and unpredictable itinerary. "Where are you going Eduardo?" I asked. "I'm going where my legs will take me, wandering erringly through this great big world of my God", he repeated. And smiled.

"The crossing is dangerous", said Rosa (1974, p.410), "but it is life". Ha, it is life, Eduardo seems to teach us, that is crossing, unable to cling exclusively to the powers that conform to it, to the biopolitics that want to achieve everything. Eduardo makes up a crossing with its dangers, uncertainties, escapes, flights, vacillations; in his wanderings. The terms used by him – and by many of my interlocutors[6] – are significant: go astray, vagrancy, flee, escape and err. If the language of affections was used to describe how AIDS patients are transformed into the "junk of the world," as I have shown in my ethnography (Pereira 2004), the terms used to describe these moments of *in-between*, moments of wandering, are those of displacement, of movement. Taking this semantic field seriously could lead us to conclude that subjectivities are also located in that which exceeds and escapes the norms, and that even under the action of biopowers over bodies and souls, something always slips, seeps and escapes.

---

[6] Only after the fieldwork was I able to understand the importance of mobility and transit for many of my interlocutors, which explains, for example, the population variance in the shelter – which at certain times, meant up to 50 fewer people (Pereira 2004).

Modernities

The theories on biopolitics alluded to in this text appear to revolve around the definition of modernity. As we have seen, if Foucault (1978, 2003, 2008) thinks modernity is linked to the entrance of life in history, for Agamben (2004a, b), modern biopolitics does not arise with modernity, since the modern state only elucidates and highlights the link between power and bare life; the most striking feature of modern life is that the state of exception is becoming the rule. Esposito (1998, 2002, 2004), in turn, argues that it is precisely in modernity that the immunization paradigm is established as structure. The discussion of biopower and biopolitics is therefore consubstantial with the understanding of what modernity is. Notwithstanding, who is included and who is outside of these conceptions of modernity? And yet, do not these theories, with their assumptions of modernity, in effect discourse about themselves while universalizing their own theoretical assumptions?

When he related modernity to an age where death no longer bludgeons life in the West, Foucault was aware of the Eurocentric character of his narrative (Butler 2001).[7] In the same paragraph that says, "Western man was gradually learning what it means to be a living species in a living world, to have a body, conditions of existence, probabilities of life, an individual and collective welfare", Foucault (1978, p.142).[8] This author also remembers that "outside the Western world, famine exists, on a greater scale than ever; and the biological risks confronting the species are perhaps greater, [...]" Foucault (1978, p.143). Contemplating these unequal contexts, we may ask: and in Brazil, what are the historical social conditions regarding the era of biopower in the West?

Unable to dwell too much on this historical social context, I would simply like to remember that when it comes to health, Machado et al. (1978) argued that the Portuguese administration was not characterized by the organization of social space in the pursuit to combat the causes of illness, acting rather negatively. In fact, concludes Machado, health had not formed part of the colonial project. Until the arrival of the Portuguese Court in Brazil, asserted Escorel and Teixeira (2008), the few existing medical doctors attended only the highest strata of the population of large cities. Only from 1808, were the first public health authorities created in the country, tasked primarily with licensing and monitoring the records of those who dedicated themselves to the healing arts and with inspectorships to prevent new diseases from arriving in the coastal towns (Gurgel 2008). By the mid nineteenth century, faced with several epidemics, a centralization of imperial power occurred that undertook a reform of the health services; during this period, however, state action

---

[7] Biopower and biopolitics are linked to the idea of governmentality. And, here also, the approaches of Foucault on the theme do not refer to forms of government outside a Western context. Governmentality thus appears as a product of modern Europe (Inda 2005, p.12). See also Pels (1997).

[8] Butler (2001, p. 13) challenges this "illusory construction" of death being expelled from Western modernity, left behind as a historical possibility, as something foreign to the West. It is, she says, a "ghost story to liberate modernity from death".

in health care was limited to the hospitalization of the severely ill in lazarettos and makeshift infirmaries and admission of the insane in the Hospice instituted by the Emperor. Hospitals were the responsibility of philanthropic entities. By the beginning of the twentieth century, nothing much had changed since the end of the Empire.[9]

However, the most frightening data are those concerning the living conditions of blacks. Miskolci (2012, p.9) indicates that, in 1872, "life expectancy in Brazil was 27 years, but only 18 for slaves". If a slave, from a group of forty, survived 10 years of work, he would notice that all the others had been killed by disease, torture or suicide. In general, official proposals regarding health care for slaves were rare; and fewer still were accompanied by measures that were not even fulfilled (Porto 2006). Porto (2006) found that concerns for medical care for the slave labour force were nonexistent. Considering this scenario, in these parts, there was no way of contemplating that which Foucault envisaged for the West when setting out a definition of biopower: probabilities of life and health.[10]

It is true that Foucault was not a historian – though his material and his manner of working were historical – rather he was a genealogist. However, the juxtaposition of these histories, these disparate frameworks, reminds me of the text by Edward Said on *Mansfield Park*, by Jane Austen. The narration of the work of Austen is situated between the eighteenth and nineteenth centuries. Said (1989, 1993) affirms that the narrator in *Mansfield Park* explores the everyday life of a social order imagined to be perfect, depisting the moral landscape that sustains it. The commitment to verisimilitude in the description of English society – with its class divisions, marriages of convenience, futile people and others who are ambitious and of little character – causes slavery to emerge in the narrative, albeit timidly: while the characters discuss how to transform that provincial mansion into an idyllic place, the master of the house has to travel hastily to the Caribbean in order to quell a slave rebellion on one of his plantations. Life in *Mansfield Park* is sustained by slavery. Said then concludes that, even as the holder of supposedly universal values, the colonizers cannot remove what is impure or ugly from their narratives.

The works of the empire, argues Carvalho (1998), "are born monstrous," because they cannot eliminate the semiotic trail of the dominated group. Proposing an analytic movement similar to Said, we can place the bodies with probabilities of life in the West and juxtapose these with black bodies in the tropics. But to what extent and in what manner are the first bodies related to precarious bodies of the tropics?

Postcolonial studies warn that the historical social framework delineated in the West is a product of the close relationship established with Others not considered modern. This confrontational relationship with their Others is actually constitutive of Western modernity (Mignolo 2003). Life was able to arise in Western history

---

[9] This chapter only traces a very general overview of health in the period in question. The characteristics described here, however, are present in virtually all the literature on the period, as observed in: Bertolli Filho (1996), Freire (1989), Gurgel (2008), Miranda (2004), Porto (2006). For a discussion on medicine and medical institutions, see Luz (1982, 1986).

[10] For a more detailed discussion on the slave system health, see Porto (2006).

because the West emerged in a particular conformation: modernity is the product of the possibilities that open to the "centrality" of Europe and the allocation of other cultures as its "periphery" (Dussel 1992, 2005). Colonial enterprise is a prerequisite for the formation of Western modernity, by conferring cumulative advantages that produce a superiority, largely the fruit of the accumulation of wealth and knowledge (Quijano 2005).

Thus, the entrance of life in history in the West occurs under, and is a condition of, the colonial action itself. Read from here in the tropics, Western modernity itself arises under the sign of colonization, a dramatic framework in which the emergence of life and the power of producing life in the West were born under the mantle of exploitation. Health and life expectancy in the West are not only simultaneous with precarious bodies of the tropics, but dependent on them.

The history of Foucault concerning the emergence of life in history and formulations that followed it – like those of Agamben, Esposito or Rabinow – do not seem, however, to address closely these connections between Western modernity and colonial practices, accomplishing a systematic silence concerning a fundamental aspect of the constitution of modernity. It is also interesting to note the limited mention of race in the work of these authors, especially if we compare them to Quijano (2005), for example, who assigns race as the central hub of his entire theory, even sustaining the racialized dimension of notions of modernity. This discussion refers us to Stoler's assertions (Stoler 1995) on race and colonialism in Foucault, which I will discuss a little later.

However, unless someone creates an inventory of the scant references to the colonial question by these authors, it may be more productive to perceive this silence as linked to their involvement in their sociocultural contexts; this silence is attributed to the limits of immersing oneself in the dilemmas of western modernity.[11] The perception of these authors intimately tied to their historical social contexts means the manner of understanding the theories is altered, since given this condition the theories appear to be local products, intimately involved in private dilemmas. The concepts of biopower and its presuppositions of modernity, in its various forms, are, despite their universal pretensions, theories anchored in private, local, provincial histories.[12]

It is this locality that produces a certain distance from alternative ways of perceiving modernity itself – these are a "privilege of the periphery" that permit the postulation, as Velho (1997) has sustained, that modernity is produced simultaneously and contemporaneously in several locations, in a multiplicity of modes of relationship between the past and present. "Alternative modernities" arise from these complex production processes that place the relationship between tradition

---

[11] However, it is worth noting that these authors maintained a certain distance from discussions on colonialism, even though a solid post-colonial literature existed.

[12] On this point, Connell (2010) argues that much of what circulates as "universal theory" is strongly rooted in the sociopolitical experience of Europe. The individual experience emerges as a generic concept, acting on spaces conceived as peripheral – such spaces where the universal theory is tested and refined, but that never emerge as a locus of reflection.

and modernity in question, and that lead to the perception of aspects that are not seen as modern, or are understood as incompletely modern, as specific formations of modernity (Giumbelli 2009). Viewed from down here, modernities thus appear in a plurality of manifestations, constituting not a singular structure, rather a set of knowledges, of discursive practices with various modes of manifestation, always presenting themselves through their variants and versions (Velho 1997, 1998, 2010). This leads us to conclude that: a) a biopolitical configuration, with its assumptions of modernity, is far from being an established given structure, conformation or para-digmatic concept, rather it is an open space that needs to be cartographed; b) dis-coursing on biopolitics implies always questioning from where you are discussing it, because, though some live modernity under the emblem of triumph, others live under the sign of suspicion and of pursing (Chatterjee 2004).

Final Notes

The concerns – or set of questions and problems – that I have presented in this paper are not intended to signal the inadequacy of the concepts of biopower and biopoli-tics. Admittedly I have inquired about some of their probable limits: the conception of transcendent power that obliterates the agency of the subjects; Eurocentrism and silencing in the colonial context; the presumption of a single modernity, with uni-versal pretensions. But there also are ways to avoid these traps.

The first way is related to the possibility of contemplating life beyond biopower. Eduardo's story tells us something of modes of inhabiting the world, narrated through powerful metaphors of displacement, of wanderings. Many researchers have invoked Deleuze to indicate that, rather than an exclusive focus on rigid abstract fields, perhaps it would be better to perceive society as something that flows and escapes, composed of "lines of flight" and that turns to subjectivities that exceed, resist and evade. But, even Foucault could be thought of in this sense. In a text in which he comments on the work of Canguilhem, Foucault (1994) makes life appear as something that is capable of error. He removes life from the field of con-sciousness to encounter it on the edge of the illness and anomaly, "with an intensity against which the course of mundane existence pales" (Giorgi and Rodríguez 2009, p.33). Contrary to the arrangements of biopower over life, the notion of "life as error" acquires an affirmative sense. And here again, I record the itinerary that I fol-lowed with Eduardo and his displacements, between error and wanderings. Wandering is related to displacement and to error. "Erring" means walking aim-lessly, peregrinating, roving and making mistakes. Wandering is, according to Aurélio's Dictionary, the quality, condition, or habit of wandering. Whereas errant is one who errs, who strays; a bum; a vagrant, a nomad, a wanderer. The semantic field that involves transitions between these terms transits between fault, error, devi-ation and crossing. In the relationship with error and deviation – which is not indi-vidual or collective; which is body but exceeds it – the virtuality of the living makes it possible to think of alternative ways of inhabiting the world.

Final Notes

The second form examines about how to relate below the line of the Equator with these theories of biopolitics. Stoler (1995) also signalized Foucault's Eurocentrism, elaborating a narrative in which sex heralded the end of the era of the reign of death with the emergence of biopower, but hardly addressed colonial, imperial and racial issues. Stoler makes us aware of the power of Foucault's analysis, despite this silence. Executing a movement similar to that which I tried to accomplish here, she inquires whether the racial and sexual configurations of the empire were constitutive rather than peripheral and responds in the affirmative, concluding that race and sexuality share their emergence with the bourgeois order in the early nineteenth century. Stoler then questions whether, in the context of the Europe of the 1970s, Foucault could have written a history of racism in a political environment in which racial identity had no political force, and in which no strategic space for race existed (Stoler 1995, p.23). Stoler's movement, therefore, is to provincialize Europe, placing Foucault's formulations (and limits) in their historical social context; and from this place, provincialized, the author of *Discipline and Punish* (*Suveiller et Punir*) helps us contemplate the intricate relationships between race, sexuality and colonial difference (Chakrabarty 2000). Stoler's movement is that of rupture and recovering Foucault.

Indeed, the challenge that these forms put forward is to break with a thought – the transcendent form of power that controls everything, and that is anchored in a vision of modernity guarded by universal abstracts produced by Western modernity – and simultaneously "recover"[13] its power. Thus, the problem is not that my interlocutors do not have something of *homo sacer*, nor that hyperpreventive practices (Castiel 2010) do not mimic Esposito's immunization paradigm, much less that we should pay no attention to strategies for governing life or for "emerging forms of life" (Fischer 2003). The problem is in taking these theories as simply "applicable" to realities other than those that produced them, decontextualizing them from their locale of enunciation. And the great provocation is to utilize these concepts, while subverting them, from shared/interlaced stories originating in the (post) colonial context – the colonial difference as part of the definition of biopolitics. It is, therefore, about breaking with Eurocentric hegemony and making the most of the concepts formulated there.

Biopolitics (and biopower) then emerges as a vast field to be studied through ethnography. Clearly it is not enough to add local stories and stir. It is important that the experiences from down here affect, in the strong sense of the term, the conceptual framework itself, and thus, it can be modified, transformed. The challenge resides in verifying how these theories with their power and limits, which are being handled by us, can be renewed, rewritten, recreated from the margins and, to use an expression that is dear to us, devoured, here, in the heat of the tropics.

---

[13] I use the terms "rupture/break" and "recover" considering the analysis of Velho (2012) in the work of Stoler (1995).

References

Agamben, G. (2004a). Homo sacer: o poder soberano e a vida nua. In *Belo Horizonte: UFMG*.

Agamben, G. (2004b). *Estado de exceção*. São Paulo: Boitempo.

Agier, M. (2002). *Aux bords du monde, les réfugiés*. Paris: Flammarion.

Appadurai, A. (2009). *O medo ao pequeno número: ensaio sobre a geografia da raiva*. São Paulo: Iluminuras.

Bastos, C. (1999). *Global responses to aids: science in emergency*. Bloomington: Indiana University Press.

Bauman, Z. (1998). *Globalization: the human consequences*. Cambridge: Polity Press.

Bertolli Filho, C. (1996). *História da saúde pública no Brasil*. São Paulo: Ática.

Butler, J, (2001). La cuestión de la transformación social. In: Butler, J.E.B. Gernsheim and L. Puigvert, orgs., *Mujeres y transformaciones sociales*, Barcelona: El Roure, 7–30.

Campbell, T. (2006). Bios, immunity, life: The thought of Roberto Esposito. *Diacritics, 36*(2), 2–22.

Castiel, L. (2010). Risco e hiperprevenção: o epidemiopoder e a promoção de saúde como prática biopolítica com formato religioso. In: R. P. Nogueira, org., *Determinação social da saúde e reforma sanitária*. Rio de Janeiro: Cebes, 161–179.

Castro, E. (2009). *Vocabulário de Foucault: um percurso pelos seus temas, conceitos e autores*. Belo Horizonte: Autêntica.

Chakrabarty, D. (2000). *Provincializing Europe: postcolonial thought and the historical difference*. New Jersey: Princeton University Press.

Chatterjee, P. (2004). Nossa modernidade. In *Colonialismo, modernidade e política* (pp. 43–65). Salvador: UFBA/CEAO.

Connell, R. (2010). *Southern theory: The global dynamics of knowledge in social science*. Cambridge: Polity Press.

de Carvalho, J. J. (1998). O olhar etnográfico e a voz subalterna. *Horizontes Antropológicos, 8*, 182–198.

Dean, M. (1999). Governmentality: power and rule in modern society. In *Search PhilPapers*. London.

Dussel, E. (1992). *1492: el encubrimiento del otro. Hacia el origen del mito de la modernidad*. Madrid: Nueva Utopía.

Dussel, E. (2005). Europa, modernidade e eurocentrismo. In: E. Lander, org., *A colonialidade do saber: eurocentrismo e ciências sociais. Perspectivas latino-americanas*. Buenos Aires: Clacso, 55-70. Colección Sur Sur.

Escorel, S. and Teixeira, L.A. (2008). História das políticas de saúde no Brasil de 1822 a 1963: do império ao desenvolvimentismo populista. In: L. Giovanella et al., org., *Políticas e Sistemas de Saúde no Brasil*. Rio de Janeiro, Fiocruz, 333–384.

Esposito, R. (1998). *Communitas: origene e destino della comunitá*. Torino: Enaudi.

Esposito, R. (2002). *Immunitas: protezione e negazione della vita*. Torino: Enaudi.

Esposito, R. (2004). *Bíos: biopolitica e filosofia*. Torino: Einaudi.

Esposito, R. (2006). Special issue to Esposito: an overview of the Italian philosopher's work. *Journal Diacritics*, (2), 36.

Fassin, D. (2000). Entre politiques de la vie et politiques du vivant. *Anthropologie et Sociétés, 24*(1), 95–116.

Fassin, D. (2006a). La biopolitique n'est pas une politique de la vie. *Sociologie et Sociétés, 38*(2), 35–48.

Fassin, D. (2006b). Biopolítica. In M. Russo & S. Caponi (Eds.),. orgs. *Estudos de filosofia e história das ciências biomédicas* (pp. 321–331). São Paulo: Discurso Editorial.

Fischer, M. (2003). *Emergent forms of life and the anthropological voice*. Durham: Duke University Press.

Foucault, M. (1978). *The will to knowledge: The history of sexuality*, New York, Radom House. vol. 1.

Foucault, M. (1994). La vie: l'expérience et la science. In *Dits et écrits IV* (pp. 763–776). Paris: Gallimard.

Foucault, M. (2003). *Society must be defended: Lectures at the Collège de France* (pp. 1975–1976). New York: Palgrave Macmillan.

Foucault, M. (2008). *Nascimento da biopolítica: curso dado no Collège de France (1978–1979)*. São Paulo: Martins Fontes.

Freire, J. C. (1989). *Ordem médica e norma familiar*. Rio de Janeiro: Graal.

Giorgi, G., & Rodríguez, F. (2009). Prólogo. In G. Giorgi & F. Rodríguez (Eds.),. orgs. *Ensayos sobrebiopolítica: excesos de vida* (pp. 9–34). Buenos Aires: Paidós.

Giumbelli, E. (2009). Modernidades alternativas e a antropologia nas dobras do tempo. *Numen: Revista de Estudos e Pesquisa da Religião, 9*(2), 11–37.

Gordon, C. (1991). Governmental rationality: An introduction. In G. Burchell, C. Gordon, & P. Miller (Eds.),. orgs *The Foucault effect* (pp. 1–51). Hemel Hempstead: Harvester Wheatsheaf.

Gurgel, C. (2008). *Doenças e curas: o Brasil nos primeiros séculos*. São Paulo: Contexto.

Inda, J. X. X. (2005). *Anthropologies of modernity: Foucault, governmentality and life politics*. Oxford: Blackwell.

Lazzarato, M. (2000). Du biopouvoir à la biopolitique. *Multitudes, 1*, 45–57.

Lemke, T. (2011). *Biopolitics: an advanced introduction*. New York: New York University Press.

Löwy, I. (1996). *Between bench and bedside: science, healing and interleukin-2 in a cancer ward*. Cambridge: Harvard University Press.

Luz, M. (1982). *Medicina e ordem política brasileira: políticas e instituições de saúde (1850–1930)*. Rio de Janeiro: Graal.

Luz, M. (1986). *Instituições médicas no Brasil: instituição e estratégia de hegemonia*. Rio de Janeiro: Graal.

Machado, R., et al. (1978). *Danação da norma: medicina social e constituição da psiquiatria no Brasil*. Rio de Janeiro: Graal.

Malette, S. (2006). *La gouvernementalité chez Michel Foucault*. Quebec: Université Laval.

Malkki, L. (1995). *Purity and exile: violence, memory and national cosmology among Hutu refugees*. Chicago: The University of Chicago Press.

Mignolo, W. (2003). *Histórias locais, projetos globais: colonialidade, saberes subalternos e pensamento liminar*. S.R. de Oliveira, trad., Belo Horizonte: UFMG.

Miranda, C.A. (2004). *A arte de curar nos tempos da Colônia: limites e espaços de cura*. Recife: Fundação de Cultura da cidade de Recife.

Miskolci, R. (2012). *O desejo da nação: masculinidade e branquitude no Brasil finissecular*. São Paulo: Annablume.

Napier, D. (2003). *The age of immunology: conceiving a future in an alienating world*. Chicago: The University of Chicago Press.

Pelbart, P. P. (2003). *Vida capital: ensaios de biopolítica*. São Paulo: Iluminuras.

Pels, P. (1997). The anthropology of colonialism: culture, history, and the emergency of western governmentality. *Annual Review of Anthropology, 26*, 163–183.

Pereira, P. P. G. (2003). Sucatas do mundo: Noções de contaminação e abjeção em uma instituição para portadores de aids. *Sociedade e Cultura, 4*(2), 127–147.

Pereira, P. P. G. (2004). *O terror e a dádiva*. Goiânia: Cânone.

Pereira, P. P. G. (2008). Anthropology and human rights: between silence and voice. *Anthropology and Humanism, 33*(1/2), 38–52.

Porto, A. (2006). O sistema de saúde do escravo no Brasil do século XIX: doenças, instituições e práticas terapêuticas. *História Ciências Saúde Manguinhos, 13*(4), 1019–1027.

Quijano, A. (2005). Colonialidade do poder, eurocentrismo e América Latina. In: E. Lander, org., A colonialidade do saber: eurocentrismo e ciências sociais. *Perspectivas latino americanas*. Buenos Aires: Clacso, 227–278.

Rabinow, P. (1999). Sujeito e governamentalidade: clementos do trabalho de Michel Foucault. In *Antropologia da razão* (pp. 27–55). Rio de Janeiro: Relume-Dumará.

Rabinow, P., & Dreyfus, H. (1995). *Michel Foucault, uma trajetória filosófica: para além do estruturalismo e da hermenêutica*. Rio de Janeiro: Forense Universitária.

Rabinow, P., & Rose, N. (2006). *O conceito de biopoder hoje. Política e Trabalho* (Vol. 24, pp. 27–57). Revista de Ciências Sociais.

Rapp, R. (2000). *Testing women, testing the fetus: the social impact of amniocentesis in America*. New York: Routledge.

Rosa, J. G. (1974). *Grande sertão: veredas*. Rio de Janeiro: J. Olympio.

Rose, N. (2007). *The politics of life itself: biomedicine, power, and subjectivity in the twenty-first century*. Princeton: Princeton University Press.

Said, E. (1989). Jane Austen and the empire. In T. Eagleton (Ed.), *Raymond Williams: critical perspectives* (pp. 150–156). Boston: Northeastern University Press.

Said, E. (1993). *Culture and imperialism*. London: Chatto & Windus.

Stoler, A. L. (1995). *Race and the education of desire: foucault's history of sexuality and the Colonial order of things*. Durham: Duke University Press.

Velho, O. (1997). Globalização: antropologia e religião. *Mana, 3*(1), 133–154.

Velho, O. (1998). O que a religião pode fazer pelas ciências sociais? *Religião e Sociedade, 19*(1), 9–17.

Velho, O. (2010). A religião é um modo de conhecimento? *Plura. Revista de Estudos de Religião, 1*(1), 3–37.

Velho, O. (2012). *Ciencias Sociales en el siglo XXI: legados, conceptos y controversias*. [Online]. Available at: http://www.acsrm.org/interactivo/fscommand/OtavioVelho.pdf. (Acessed: 22 Jun 2018).

Chapter 3
Queer in the Tropics

The expression *queer* can used as a form of self-designation; that is, both repeating and reiterating homophobic voices that signal the abjection of anything denominated as *queer*, but also decontextualizing these voices from this universe of enunciation and attributing positive values to the term, transforming it into a proud form of manifesting difference. This usage may occasion an inversion in the chain of repetition that confers power to preexisting authoritarian structures, an inversion of this constitutive historicity. Something new, then, arises, from this process, announcing the irreducibility and expressing the bothersome and non-assimilable difference of bodies and souls that dare to make themselves present (Pereira 2006, p. 469).

I begin this chapter with this epigraph as an attempt to resume and highlight the slew of possibilities that *queer* theory opens. When I wrote the above words, I wanted to emphasize the potency of the political gesture that juxtaposed the decontextualization of the initial homophobic assertion; that is, the enunciation of difference, the positivity conferred to the term *queer*, and the probability of inverting the chain of repetition. In the work that follows below, I aim to problematize both the potency and also the possible limits of *queer* theory when it travels to the tropics.

Teresa de Lauretis was the first to use the word *queer* in a theoretical context, but she was also one of its first critics: in her mind, *queerness* had transformed into a conceptually empty creation of the cultural industry (De Lauretis 1991). Meanwhile, writing from Australia, Connell (2010) claimed that the science of the metropolis continues to be exported in a sort of commerce that includes both Foucault and *queer* theory itself. And it is this – our risk of repeating in the Global South what is already outdated in the Global North – that alerts us to the need to take seriously investigations of *queer* theory's potentials when it travels to the tropics.

Considering the risk, we can inquire: are we facing another theory that moves from the center to the periphery (and that is bound to rewrite, in different colors, this center-periphery divide)? Does the persistence of the English-language term *queer* signal a geopolitics of knowledge in which certain people formulate theories to be applied by others? How, then, can we translate the expression "*queer*?". In other words, how can we think *queerly* in the tropics?

© The Author(s), under exclusive license to Springer Nature Switzerland AG 2019   29
P. P. G. Pereira, *Queer in the Tropics*, SpringerBriefs in Sociology,
https://doi.org/10.1007/978-3-030-15074-7_3

Queer Theory

The movement that the self-designating use of *queer* allows is sometimes understood as a variation on the word as adjective: an alteration focused on the form of perceiving the adjective's qualities. This modification is located in the transition from a quality considered to be negative to another positive one. The alteration enunciates and reiterates *queer* bodies as possibilities, producing a shock that introduces, into the field of the possible, a difference that cannot be assimilated; there in lies its eminently transgressive character. This transgression is produced by a *political gesture* that affirms differences and inscribes strange bodies in contemporary scenarios: it is a *gesture* that confers visibility to invisible people, highlighting the "strangers within society" (Butler 1990, 2005; Louro 2001; Miskolci 2009). But it is also more than this.

There is another dimension to this process, a dimension that frequently remains unperceived by analyzes that focus on verifying what the adjective *queer* used to be and what it has become, but that forget the movement of the word itself. *Queer* supplants the identifying act accepted as such, as well as its reifying effects on identities. In the unstable action of transforming an injury into a proud form of self-designation, what stands out is the word's movement. *Queer* is therefore an adjective (or a noun), but also – more appropriately – a verb that designs risky actions and dislocations, and that delineates multiple trajectories of unstable, provisional, and split bodies. The performative act causes change, and it is this change that is bothersome and unsettling, not only because it alters the subjects who enunciate it, but also because it introduces the possibility of transformation. The multiplicity of drag, trans, and gay bodies signals this possibility of transformation. Therefore, it is not the safety of the operated body, finally consonant with its gender identity, that *queerness* proposes; rather, it carries with it the instability of bodies that do not conform. Bodies, surgeries, prostheses, sexual practices, transsexuals, drag personas, and *travetis* arise in the word's movement, denouncing the precariousness of that which announces itself as the norm and installs itself as a coherent form of life, a privileged path.

We can therefore speak of reappropriations and conversions in the construction of *queer* bodies, and of a reappropriation of the disciplines of knowledge and power relating to the sexes, as well as a re-articulation and conversion of the technologies of production of these sexes. *Queer* bodies rebel against the very construction of "normal" and "abnormal" bodies, subverting dominant norms of subjectivity. What is *queer*, then, promotes a performative power shift in discourses of the reappropriation of the production technology of abnormal bodies, and enters our contemporary scenario as the proposal of transformation in the circulation of discourses and the mutability of bodies (Preciado 2002a; Pereira 2006; 2014). It is from this place of dislocation and reconfiguration that *queerness* positions itself.

However, when described in such a generic form, and without the necessary care given to its specificities, *queerness* seems – contradictorily – to cloud over differences, even though the concept itself is meant be a politics of difference. This is because generalization constrains both the variations within *queer* theory itself as well as the local histories that are simply forgotten within such generic conceptual differentiations. The utilization of a common repertory among authors, such as the struggle against compulsory heterosexuality (Rich 1993) or a position against simple binarism, among others, are characteristics that confer an aura of transgression and contestation to *queer* thinking. Based on a hasty approach, this commonality might suggest an integration of positions into a single and homogenous whole. Yet the divergences within *queer* thinking are significant; therefore, treating these positions and theories in a unified form and disregarding the specificity of each thought rescinds the power of these proposals and ideas. When removed from the context of enunciation, and without giving sufficient attention to the singularity of each theoretical *corpus*, we always run the risk of clouding over the density of *queer* propositions, which require continuous and intense self-reflective movement. This, in turn, leads to the pure and simple repetition of theories, without allowing any resistance on the part of the realities under analysis. Theory, in this case, becomes disassociated from local realities; without confrontation, we enter into a circle that induces the eternal (peripheral) repetition of (central) theories. Is this the burden of *queerness* in the tropics?

Points of Tension

In order to respond to this line of questioning and give greater direction to my discussion, I would like to comment on the work of Preciado (2008 and 2009). This choice arises because Preciado exposes and synthesizes certain points of tension within *queer* theory in a very clear way. I do not intend to linger on Preciado's texts, so I will simply aim to highlight three points that I consider central to his project: first, the centrality of new technologies of the body; second, the place of agency; and third, the power of *pharmacopornography*.

Preciado alerts us to the necessity of being attentive to new technologies of the body, and it is his perception of this necessity that leads him to signal the limits of performative gender analysis, which reduces gender to the effects of discourse. He maintains that performance theory does not give sufficient importance to specific technologies of embodiment, and that it is these very technologies that make different performative inscriptions possible (San Martín 2009). The concept of the performance of gender does not consider the biotechnological processes that allow certain performances to be considered natural, to the detriment of other performances that are understood to be unnatural. Based on this differentiation, Preciado asserts that gender is not simply a performative effect, but that it is, above all, a process of prosthetic embodiment (Preciado 2002b). These critiques are aimed at Judith Butler, in whose theories Preciado sees a centralization of the discursive dimension that produces an obliteration of the body. Preciado's *demarche* also does not leave Michel Foucault unscathed. The author of *The History of Sexuality* focused exclusively on the idea of a management of life; he did not approach the propagation of technologics of the body and of representation with greater caution, all of which implies limits to his proposals, as we will see shortly. Preciado, with the intuition of staying attentive to new technologies of the body and advancing where Foucault and Butler could not, argues that hormones are biopolitical fictions: fictions that can be consumed, digested, and embodied. Hormones are biopolitical elements that create corporal formations and integrate themselves to larger political organisms. We might there-fore think of gender as the mark of production of an agglomeration of synthetic materials, such as birth control pills; silicone; dresses; architecture and publicity codes; pornography; social spaces and their divisions; and the division of bodies into sexual organs and functions.

Beyond discussions of body and performativity, Preciado's work raises the ques-tion of the possibility of action, and of subversive political practices. Butler, in her first formulations of the theme, affirms that gender is a performative effect of repeti-tive acts (without origin or essence). Thus, all signification occurs within the space of obligation to repeat these acts and performances. Following this formulation, some researchers deduce that, because the agency of subjects is linked to the non-subjection of norms that impel repetition, it would only be reasonable to deduce that only those who disentangle themselves from chains of repetition, and who dissent from established norms, act in an effective manner. Preciado, however, thinks of agency differently, emphasizing biotechnologies and subversive potentialities. For him, subjects act through cybernetic prostheses and chemical substances. This means that prostheses and chemicals make the actions of agents possible, constitut-ing them by means of mediated actions. If, according to Butler, contemporary agents define themselves through acts, corporal gestures, and discourses, Preciado sees these agents as being characterized by the mediation between the body and biotechnology (San Martín 2009, p. 98). Preciado opts for a view that privileges political action, and that seems to withdraw from Butler's idea of the inexistence of a subject prior to norms: he attributes a contractual capacity and the status of rela-tive sovereignty to subjects within their subversive action (San Martín 2009, pp. 98–99).

Another point in Preciado's elaborations is his search to add to the theory of biopower. Foucault (1978), in the final chapter of *The Will to Knowledge*, writes of an era in which death would no longer fustigate life. The threshold of biological modernity, he writes, situates itself precisely where life enters into history, inaugu-rating an era of a bio-power. Foucault describes modernity as the indistinguishable nature between biological and political life, in which politics turns back to govern life. Based on these elaborations, Preciado argues that Foucault, as already men-tioned, does not pay enough attention to the transformations in technologies of the production of subjectivity that occurred beginning with World War II. These are the transformations that lead Preciado to propose a third regime of subjectification, a third system of knowledge-power that he calls *pharmacopornography*. Changes are located in forms of operating: in disciplinary society, technologies of subjectifica-tion control the body from the outside, like an external orthodontic-architectural apparatus. In *pharmacopornographic* society, technologies form part of the body and dilute themselves within it. Technologies convert themselves into the body, as there is no space between technology and the body (Cabral 2009; Fischer 2009; San Martín 2009). In *pharmacopornographic* society, power acts by means of molecules, silicones, neurotransmitters, and hormones, among other means. And between the validity of sexual difference as a regulatory and malleable ideal of bodies – through a medical system that acts with biochemical and bio-narrative fluxes – multiple and unforeseen opportunities open for the appropriation of these technologies and narratives, as well as for subversion.

Situated Theories

Preciado's contributions present themselves as tropes of newness and overcoming. Here, everything takes place as though something new has arisen on the theoretical horizon, surpassing previous formulations, especially those of Foucault and Butler. Looking more closely, however, we can conclude that these contributions do not present significant novelties. Donna Haraway and Teresa de Lauretis had already touched on technologies, and Butler herself sought to address the question in works following *Gender Trouble.* In terms of agency, Butler (2005) confronts the topic more directly in *Giving an Account of Oneself,* a work in which she attempts to overcome the opposition between voluntarism and determinism. In this book, Butler valorizes the inventiveness of morality, a morality that cannot be reduced to rules, laws, or values, but within which a given subject is also not entirely free to ignore these systems. Butler maintains that we are not merely the effect of discourses, as hasty constructivism might assert, because discourses and regimes of truth always constitute us at a determined price. Butler's formulations can, in this way, lead us to further interrogate Preciado's idea of agents with contractual capacity.

The proposal of a new regime of power-knowledge is even more complicated. This is both because authors such as Rose (2007) have already alerted us to the fact that biologistic molecularization is a crucial dimension of contemporary biopolitics, and also because the aforementioned proposal does not problematize the periodization that Foucault elaborates, but simply adds a new configuration to it, namely *pharmacopornography*. When Foucault related modernity to the epoch in which death no longer fustigates Western life, he was conscious of the Eurocentric character of his narrative. Yet the problem here is not only the Eurocentrism of Foucault's analysis, but also the conditions in which European bio-power emerged. The entrance of life within Western history takes place through colonizing action, and this action serves as a condition for its emergence. As read from here in the tropics, the era of bio-power (or of Western modernity) arose under the sign of colonization in a dramatic framework through which the emergence of life – and the potential of producing life in the West – was born under the mantle of exploitation. However, Foucault's narrative of the appearance of life in history, as well as Preciado's formulations, do not appear to examine these links between biopower and colonial practices more closely. Instead, they construct a systematic silence regarding a fundamental aspect of the constitution of modernity. This silence is certainly linked to these authors' involvement in their own sociocultural contexts, and must be attributed to the limits of their immersion within the dilemmas of Western modernity. Their perception, intimately linked to their sociohistorical framework, alters our own forms of understanding their theories; in this condition, they appear as local products, intimately involved in their particular dilemmas. The concepts of bio-power (in its multiple versions) and of *pharmacopornopower* are, in spite of their universal aspirations, theories anchored in specific, local, and provincial histories (Pereira 2013).

In spite of these caveats, it is worth remembering that we are discussing a work in development. Preciado's work has yet to be tested, and it may yet overcome much of what can be considered "problematic" in its theoretical production. However, I find Preciado's universal aspirations to be a more delicate problem. He writes, "we are entering an era in which the techno-molecular control of gender will extend itself to everything and everyone," and declares, "the twenty-first century will be the century of the *pharmacopornographic* production and control of masculinity" (Preciado 2008, p. 127). Preciado attempts to make theoretical modes of articulation and politics universal when, in fact, they come from the Global North from which he himself speaks. It falls to us, then, to *apply*, in the tropics, theories with universal aspirations that are formulated elsewhere. These theories do not directly confront the actual conditions through which Western bio-power emerged, since they either forget colonial actions or approach them tangentially. Therefore, there is no way for us not to think of Preciado's texts as powerful narratives characterized by a homogeneous temporal construction that acts by obscuring the multiplicity of heterogeneous times. There is also no way to forget, as Cabral (2009) puts it, the work of manifesting a Global North that only manages to read itself, even as it collectivizes its systematic hypotheses of global reach.[1]

Local Experiences

After this discussion, we can return to asking whether *queerness* is a possible opening toward Others, and whether, here in the tropics, we have experience of other conformations, or whether, instead, we are destined to be the objects of *pharmacopornopower*. Could certain insurgent experiences and forms of knowledge exist that might allow us to come closer to the inquiries about *queerness* formulated at the beginning of this chapter?

When I asked myself these questions, I thought immediately of Cida, a *travesti* with whom I involved myself while carrying out an ethnographic study in a shelter for AIDS patients (Pereira 2004). In May 1998, I met Cida, who was then 44 years old, in a shelter on the periphery of Brasília, where she had lived for 3 years. Based on her discretion and her economy of gestures, she seemed to me to be from the

---

[1] The option of a critique of universalism does not refer to all *queer* theory, but it applies to some of its formulations. For a critique of universalism, see Muñoz (1999, 2006).

backcountry. And, in fact, she was born in a small town in the interior of the state of Minas Gerais, in the Vale do Rio Doce region. It was only through concerted effort that I managed to learn anything about her life. One afternoon, however, Cida spoke more extensively and, in her syncopated prose, told me her story.

Cida had long perceived herself to be different from other boys, and had felt firsthand the prejudice and violence that stemmed from others' discomfort with her choices and actions. Throughout our encounters, she made it clear that her life was a path of self-knowledge. As a child, she learned to observe and imitate the women she admired, and she attempted to make her body "work" so that it would act as she desired. Several times, she told me details about fabrics, dresses, and parties, in narratives that moved from admiration to desire to inadequacy. In the midst of this whirlwind of information, she also told me the story of a doctor that her family trusted. This doctor perceived that "this boy was different", and he initiated practices that changed Cida's body. According to Cida, "[the doctor] began to harass me. He would be alone with me, and began to do things. He gave me medicine, and my little breasts began to grow. I was twelve years old when I made love to him". From that point, her body was so altered that she had to leave small-town Minas Gerais. At first, she moved to Belo Horizonte (The state capital of Minas Gerais), and it was there that she discovered herself to be a *travesti*: "I became a *travesti*. I was beautiful! Later, I left to make a living. I worked for a long time on the streets in Belo Horizonte, Italy, and in Spain". And it was while Cida was in Europe that she started using heavy drugs, and also where she contracted HIV.

Cida's illness led her to return to the backcountry. She tried to make herself unnoticeable in the city where she was born, cutting her hair short and "not standing out", "pretending to be a man". However, she was not successful, and so she had to move once again. She also found herself unable to "make a living" on the streets, as her illnesses began to modify her appearance. Without a means of survival, without help from people around her, and without support from her close family members, the only alternative that Cida found was to live in the shelter where I met her.

Cida's story reminded me of the story that Preciado tells of herself in *Testo Yonqui*. Certain similarities are obvious: both Cida and Preciado underwent physical changes, lived in big cities, manifested their dissident sexualities, and were born in small towns in the backcountry. The differences between them, however, are also quite numerous. Preciado (2008, p. 77) writes: "I inhabit distinct Western megacities". The verb "inhabit" is dear to a philosopher, as it indicates a *decision* to form ties to these places, as seen, for example, in Heidegger (1986). Cida, in spite of being well travelled, never abandoned her hometown, which has continued to accompany her in her gestures and her mode of speech. During her travels throughout Europe, her contact with other languages was marked by a sense of inadequacy: "I made it through, but I always thought that I was very stupid with languages", Cida told me when I asked if she spoke Italian or Spanish. "I'm from the interior, I even speak Portuguese wrong and with an accent", she added, underscoring her perception of herself as lacking ability.

Preciado (2008, p. 77), on the other hand, writes: "I transit between three languages, none of which I consider to be mine, nor to be foreign", and writes jubilantly of the "singular pleasure of writing in English, in French, in Spanish, of walking from one language to another". In this sense, Cida is closer to Anzaldúa (1999), for whom "when you live on the border … you are stupid". Preciado (2008, p.77) regards Burgos – a city where "the girls" he "loved in [his] childhood" are now married, have children, and "struggle actively against relaxing the muscles in their necks" – with distrust, and with a certain antipathy.

Here, we see in Preciado's work a narrative that is far from what Das (2007) constructed in telling the stories of Manjit and Asha, and equally distant from the admiring gaze that Cida always took on when she spoke of women at dance balls in the country, and the delicate manner in which she spoke about "women's ways". We have here a philosopher who speaks of the big cities that he inhabits in Europe and the United States, and a *travesti* who has travelled to various cities, and who now lives in a shelter for AIDS patients in Brazil. Preciado, who self-administers hormones, can handle refined theories, and who uses the word *queer*. Cida, on the other hand, is a strange, eccentric body, disfigured by AIDS, but who can also handle sophisticated theories…

After almost a year of conversations – by which time I was already very familiar with the universe of the shelter in which she lived – I had an encounter with Cida that stood out from the rest. This was the day on which she told me a fascinating story about her religious life: she was a "*daughter*" of *Iansã*,[2] and an *Umbanda* initiate. She went to an *Umbanda* center whenever she could, and it was there that she felt supported. The ills that had befallen Cida, which made no sense to her, diminished when she perceived that she could still "work her body". Because the shelter where she lived controlled its residents' movements, Cida "escaped" at night to an *Umbanda* center located nearby, on a dirt road in a simple, brightly-colored house on Brasília's periphery. There, she danced and "spun", and was possessed by a *Pomba-gira*.[3] "I have AIDS, I have nothing in life, but I'll die as a *batuqueira*"[4] she told me. I recorded this conversation in my fieldwork notebook, and spoke about it to specialists in Afro-Brazilian religions, but I never stopped to examine Cida's formulations, in part because I felt uncomfortable approaching a theme of which I did not have extensive knowledge. At that time, I could not bring myself closer to the theory that Cida was presenting to me, a theory whose density and relevance I only managed to perceive much later.

In any event, I thought about Cida's experiences constantly. I recalled that her body was the object of hormone-based technologies, but that these had been administered by a small-town doctor linked to her family. I remembered that her desire to

---

[2] Iansã is a female warrior *orixá* (divinity) associated with the wind, storms, sorcery, and lightning. Iansã, Oxum, Iemanjá, and Oxalá are deities in the pantheons of various Afro-Brazilian religions. (T.N.)

[3] The *Pomba-gira*, a spirit worshipped in diverse Candomblé and Umbanda traditions, is a popular figure in Brazil. Its origins are in Candomblé practices, and its worship is composed of interlinking African and European traditions. The *Pomba-gira* is considered to be a feminine *Exu*. *Exu*, in Candomblé traditions of Yoruba origin (including Ketu, Efan, and Pernambuco Nagô) is the *orixá* who serves as a Messenger between humans and *orixás* (Prandi 1996, p. 139).

[4] In this usage, *batuqueira* refers to a woman who dances to drumming.

recreate corporal performances was connected to the performances of traditional women from the country; it was not by chance that Cida, while surrounded by modesty and moderation, dreamed of plunging necklines and shiny baubles. I remembered that she was a well-travelled person, but she preserved her rural accent and the ways of small-town folks; it seemed that the little town where she was born always accompanied her in her travels through her body and through the world. Hers was a body composed of dreams of sequins, organza, and parties; of mimetic performances of the postures, gestures, and behaviors of women from Brazil's backcountries; of hormones administered by a family doctor; of silicone administered by back-alley *"pumpers"* and surgeons; of voyages where she exchanged experiences and bodily fluids; of intensive experiences with drugs; of a debilitated immune system; of infirmities that transformed her body; of illnesses that led her to a shelter for AIDS patients. This body was "worked through" in the drumbeats of *Umbanda* rituals. The body of a daughter of *Iansã*, an *orixá* who was once a man and had transformed into a woman, who has the body of a woman and masculine determination, who rejects maternity and is a warrior and defender of justice (Segato 1995).

Bodies in Transit

In 2011, 10 years after the conclusion of my ethnography, I began to supervise Martha Souza, a doctoral student who was researching the experiences of *travestis* in the Public Health System in Santa Maria, a city in the state of Rio Grande do Sul. Martha quickly found a gap in the program's accompaniment of its patients that showed its inadequacy in offering services to *travestis*. Yet Martha also found other forms of caring for and welcoming these patients that she had not anticipated. Out of the roughly fifty *travesties* that she accompanied in her fieldwork, nearly forty regularly visited *"saints' houses"*. They called themselves Catholic, but they also practiced "Afro-Brazilian" religions. Martha's research, which focused initially on the boardinghouses and other residences where these *travestis* lived, as well as on locations for practicing prostitution and on local clinics, wound up also focusing on *"saints' houses"*, the majority of which were located in Santa Maria's poor neighborhoods.

Martha discovered a much richer reality than she could have imagined, inhabited by noteworthy characters like Xuca, a roughly 30-year-old *travesti*, whose *"head saint"*[5] was *Iemanjá* and whose *"body saint"* was Oxalá. Xuca is also "Father Ricardo", a male priest (*"father-of-a-saint"*),[6] and she is married to another priest

---

[5] In Afro-Brazilian religions, each initiate has *orixás* that protect the head and the body. During rituals, these initiates "make their heads," and care for their *orixás*.

[6] A "father-of-a-saint" or "mother-of-a-saint" is the central authority figure within a *terreiro*, responsible for leading both religious events and other activities. They express the will of the orixá who commands the terreiro. They are also called caretakers, because their task is to care for the saints, the terreiro, and for initiates (the children-of-a-saint).

who is a candidate for Santa Maria's city council. Martha also met characters like Joy and Carol: the first is the "dean" of the city's *travestis*, roughly 54 years old and a respected female priestess ("mother-of-a-saint"); while the second, Carol, is the daughter of Father Ricardo (Xuca). Iemanjá is the "head saint" of all three; all three are blonde, take hormones, and have had silicone implants. Their bodies, like the bodies of other *travestis* who frequent *"saints' houses"*, have absorbed hormones; plastic surgery; long and painstaking hair implants; and facial hair removal with lasers, tweezers, wax, or safety razors.

In Santa Maria,[7] the mothers- and fathers-of-saints say that they "consider three sides:" "nation", *Umbanda*, and *Quimbanda*. Martha's research shows that *travestis* prefer to participate in *Quimbanda* rituals, in which, as they say, *"Exu[8] reigns"*; these rituals allow them to be possessed by *Pomba-giras* and to dance to the sound of *batuque*, as well as to execute physical performances or relate to female *orixás*. On certain occasions, especially feasts for the *orixás*, the *travestis* dress in very feminine clothes, and go to the *"saints' houses"* at night, thereby giving up their professional activities, typically prostitution. Once there, they go directly to the spaces reserved for *Quimbanda*. Accompanied by *batuque* drumming, they go into trance, possessed by the *Pomba-gira*: the spirit of a woman (rather than an *orixá*) who was a prostitute in her life, a woman capable of dominating men through her sexual prowess, a woman who loved luxury, money, and pleasure.

The framework of Afro-Brazilian religion is a complex one that involves contact between different religious perspectives; characters who handle sophisticated, mythological forms of knowledge, and who construct a grammar of gender and sexuality that removes itself from compulsory heterosexuality; the technological reconstructions of bodies; as well as ritual performances centered on bodies and made up of a movement that evokes and produces these same bodies. This framework, as I have mentioned, allows a *travesti* who has already passed through all kinds of technological interventions to produce a feminine body, and to call herself by a feminine name. This is the case regardless of whether she is a *"father-of-a-saint"*, or whether *Iemanjá* is her "head saint"; myths, technology, and rituals allow her to invent new forms of being in the world. In fact, we can say here that man-bodies

---

[7] *Travestis* in Santa Maria are inserted in Batuque and Quimbanda traditions. Batuque, in addition to serving as a term used to designate percussive rhythms in general, is also a religion that worships twelve *orixás*; it is divided into different "sides" or "nations", and the Nago language serves as its liturgical base (Oro, 2012). Throughout my research, fathers- and mothers-of-saints explained what they recognize as three distinct "sides": "nation", Umbanda, and Quimbanda/Crossed Line (*Linha Cruzada*). See also Corrêa (1992). As Oro (1994, 2002) explains, Batuque venerates *orixás* exclusively; Umbanda adds *caboclos* and *pretos-velhos* (ancestral spirits of African descent); while *Linha Cruzada* joins together all of these entities along with *exus* and mythical women spirits like the *pomba-giras*. As we can see, Afro-Brazilian religions contain numerous possibilities that can be adjusted according to given situations. (Goldman 2009, p. 110) For more on Afro-Brazilian religions in Rio Grande do Sul, see Correa (1994) and Oro (2002, 2008). For more on batuque (drumming) in Rio Grande do Sul, see Braga (1998) and Correa (1992).

[8] *Exu* is the *orixá* who serves as a messenger between humankind and the world of the *orixás*. *Pomba-giras* and *Exus* are associated with transgression. *Pomba-giras* are female *Exus*. For more on this topic, see Augras (1989), Contins and Goldman (1984), Meyer (1993) andTrindade (1985).

and woman-bodies are not tied to biology. Instead, they reinvent themselves and make us question whether the terms "man" and "woman" can adequately be juxtaposed to the term "body". They make us question the direct link between gender and sex. No matter how we think about this context, it seems very clear that an insistent search exists for different grammars of bodies.

Different Bodies, Distinct Mediators

My own fieldwork, as well as the experience that I am sharing with Martha Souza in Santa Maria, are both consistent with the analyses of many different researchers' examinations of sexuality in Afro-Brazilian religions (Birman 1985, 1995, 2005; Fry 1977, 1982; Leão Teixeira 2000a; Santos 2008; Segato 1995).[9] Segato (1995), reflecting on *Xangô* in Recife, argues that *Xangô* aims to systematically liberate categories of familial relation, personality, gender, and sexuality from biological determinations, and to dislocate matrimony from its central place in social structure.[10] This aim may be accompanied by the practice of attributing "man saints" and "woman saints" indistinguishably to both men and women as personality types; by the treatment that myths give to the male and female roles of *orixás*; by the critical vision that *Xangô* members hold in relation to the rights derived from maternal blood relations; by the importance given to the fictitious family formed by the

---

[9] Conner and Sparks (2004) have the merit of being the first authors to point to the relationship between *queerness* and African tradition in the Americas. Their work includes an examination of Yoruba *orixás* and the diasporic tradition of these spirits in Brazil.

[10] Although the ethnographic references in the text, as they relate to religious experiences, are specific to the city of Santa Maria, I also utilize references to Recife's Xangô tradition, to the nationwide practice of Umbanda, to Candomblé in São Paulo and in Rio de Janeiro, and to Quimbanda in Porto Alegre and Santa Maria. Oro (1994) gives an overview of Afro-Brazilian religions by dividing these religions into three models of ritualistic expression. The first of these is distinguished by worship of the orixás; it privileges mythological, symbolic, linguistic, doctrinal, and ritualistic elements from the Bantu and Nagô traditions. This group includes Candomblé in Bahia, Xangô in Recife, Batuque in Rio Grande do Sul, and Casa de Mina in Maranhão. Candomblé is the Afro-Brazilian religion of big cities in Brazil's northeastern coast, especially in Salvador and Recife. The denomination "Candomblé" first became generalized in Bahia; in Recife, the designation "Xangô" is more prevalent. (Motta 1995; on Xangô, see Carvalho 1990) The second of these models seems to have emerged from Candomblé, mixing traditions and adapting itself to Brazil's urban life. This group includes macumba and, depending on regional variations, is also referred to as Quimbanda, Linha Negra, Black Magic (*magia negra*), Umbanda Cruzada, or Linha Cruzada. The third model is Umbanda, composed of elements of Catholic, African, Indigenous, Kardecist (Spiritist), and Asian religious traditions. In Umbanda, both religious rituals and doctrinal elements vary among different regions and places of worship, according to emphasis that local followers give to Spiritism, Asian, and African practices, among others. José Jorge de Carvalho identifies two styles of religious practice: the traditional, which is linked exclusively to African divinities and features a rigid and complex ritual; and other practices that incorporate diverse entities aside from the orixás, including caboclos, *Exus*, *preto-velhos*, and *Pomba-giras* (Carvalho 1994, p. 88). However, it is important to call attention to the regional specificities of Afro-Brazilian in different parts of the country.

"*family of [a] saint*"; and by the bisexuality of most of the sect's masculine and feminine members. In this way, *Xangô's* worldview adopts a posture of non-essentialism that operates by de-naturalizing received models of family, gender, and maternity. This sparse summary does not do justice to Segato's sophisticated arguments, but it is sufficient for the discussion that I am proposing here. Segato's analyses and the material of which I am availing myself allow me to affirm the existence of a type of operation that sustains the independence of the sphere of sexuality, thereby escaping from essential categories or rigid identities, and searching for a new grammar capable of welcoming these desires and aspirations.

This framework is not a reality without conflicts. The diversity of Afro-Brazilian religions produces distinct forms of dealing with sexuality, which range from welcoming acceptance – such as takes place among the *travestis* of Santa Maria – as well as to practices more closely linked to a binary, heterosexual logic (which must still be better described and analyzed).[11] Another important, and also conflictual, dimension is the degree to which *travestis* are involved in articulating a religious perspective. There is a type of agency that does not make claims in the way that social movements do, but that nevertheless involves itself with determined forms of religious knowledge and action, with mythology and ritual performance, and with religious theories and codices. Involvement with this universe, however, is not universal, as we can see in the distinction between initiated *travestis,* such as the *fathers- and mothers-of-saints*, and those *travestis* in Santa Maria who merely frequent *Quimbanda* rituals. In the first case, the *travestis'* religious action takes place in a differentiated language that is expressly distant from hegemonic patterns of sexuality and gender, given its immersion in this other form of knowledge, and in this other universe of values. However, in the second case, *travestis* seek to be welcomed for their dissident sexualities within a new grammar; in religion, they seek performative and moral options, options of knowledge that justify their choices, options that welcome them, and through which they can express themselves. The fathers- and mothers-of-saints notice this distinction. When asked to comment, Cláudio – a male priest – said the following:

> For example, if a *travesti* comes here for a cowry shell reading and Fernando [a priest] throws shells for him and sees that he has a male "head saint," we won't change [the saint's name]. Because the *travesti* thinks like this: I have to belong to Oxum, to Iemanjá, or to Oyá [All female *orixás*]. Because that will justify them dressing like women. Because then they'll dress like women, they'll use Oxum's things. So [they think] I must be a [female saint's] daughter. I have to be well made-up, well put together. If you want to come as a woman, come. You just have to respect the house.

---

[11] Such as separating *travestis* and assigning them to masculine spaces in the rituals. José Jorge de Carvalho, in a personal communication, reminded me that women are forbidden to sacrifice the animals offered to the *orixás*, and that they are not allowed to touch *atabaque* drums, as drumming is considered part of the masculine sphere. In Santa Maria, Father Ricardo – when asked about the topic – said that *travestis* are also men, since they "have penises", and that, therefore, they may participate in rituals that include animal sacrifice. According to him, "women need a 'science' [wisdom] to be able to kill animals. Once they have that 'science,' they can do what men do, or else they can find a man to help them". In other words, a body might be worked through the ritual *and, to a certain extent, remove itself from the division of ritual roles based on gender.*

Travestis seek to establish a relationship with the saints, as though being consecrated to a female saint justified their sexuality and femininity. *Travestis* access the *orixás*, *Exus*, and all Afro-Brazilian religious mythology as forms of thinking about physical transformations and about desire. However, a person consecrated to *Iansã*, *Iemanjá*, or *Oxum* may have to observe religious rituals dressed in feminine clothes and accessories, regardless of that person's sexual orientation. When Cláudio points out the importance of "respect[ing] the house", he is highlighting the priority given to the sacred, and to religious logic with all its rituals, codes, and myths. He is affirming that religious tradition is more complex than – and does not permit quick translations linked to – the hegemonic language of gender, sexuality, and dimorphism. Thus, the priest speaks to the logic of myth, to modes of knowledge that operate on levels other than the *travestis'* desire to make mythic language conform to their own aspirations of physical transformation.[12] Cláudio maintains that, although *travestis'* aspirations are not spurious, a religious perspective is more intricate, and more intensely sinuous.

Travestis are anxious for a new language that offers them conditions to see themselves through new lenses and at different angles, and to leave the spaces in which their bodies are treated as abject in order to arrive at other spaces in which their bodies are beautiful, and their desires legitimate. In these spaces (in "saints' houses" on unpaved streets in precarious, far-flung neighborhoods), they can dance in a state of trance, incorporating *Pomba-giras*, to the sound of batuque drumming. In this moment, they hear and intone the song:

Look: what a beautiful girl!
Look: what a beautiful girl!
It's the *Pomba-gira* Girl
Calling me from the window (repeat)
Turn, Girl, turn
I want to see you turn…
Turn, beautiful Girl,
Because *Exu* cannot desire.

This is not insignificant. The *Pomba-gira*, who is venerated in *Candomblé* and *Umbanda*, is a popular character throughout Brazil. Poor people who live in the city work with the entity to resolve afflictions related to desires and sexuality. Narratives involving the *Pomba-gira* reveal something of "the aspirations and frustrations of

---

[12] Spirit possession, which plays a central role in Afro-Brazilian religions, is a ritual phenomenon that permits practitioners to bring *orun* (the world of the *orixás*) closer to *aiê* (the human world). During possession, an *orixá* (or an *Exu*) "descends", and carries out performances to the sound of drumming made up of gestures and dance steps executed in time to ritual drumming. This possession brings *orun* and *aiê* closer, and also serves to express otherness. Cláudio calls our attention to *travestis'* utilization of religion as a form of justifying their sexual and gender identities. According to him, one must always obey religious logic, which demands practices ranging from cowry shell readings, close readings of texts, and initiation rituals, until one's "head saint" can be attributed. So it may be that the greatest practice of transit among transvestites in *Quimbanda* is one of justification through the intimate relationship that they establish with *Pomba-giras*.

large portions of the population that are very distant from an ethical and moral code based on traditional Western, Christian values" (Prandi, 1996, p. 140). There is no way to remove these bodies from their local histories.

These local histories construct different bodies, since they are articulated by different mediators. Birman (2005) makes this clear in her consideration of supernatural entities, in which she does not turn the effects and products of spirit possession into unreal phenomena, but rather accepts the agency of saints and other entities. This valorizes the point of view of mediums and fathers- and mothers-of-saints, and allows us to observe the practice of spirit possession as it interweaves humans, gods, and spirits "in webs that include sexual desires, affective bonds, and gender roles with the power differences that pass through all of these inter-relations" (Birman, 2005, p. 404). If Birman is correct, then for the *travestis* of Santa Maria, these beings are mediators to the same extent as biotechnology. These *travestis* define themselves through acts, physical gestures, and discourses; through cybernetic prosthetics and through chemical substances; but also through saints and entities. *Travestis'* bodies are different, both because they are produced by other mediators and because they are conformed by (and conform to) other subjectivities. Bodies constructed by hormones and silicone must also be "worked through batuque drumming", as Cida had already taught me.

Religion therefore offers an alternative grammar and lexicon for *travestis'* personal expression, because it is through religion that they find a mode of knowledge and a structure capable of sheltering their experiences of transit and flux, as well as a convenient lexicon for circulating in and sliding between different options of sex and gender. The *travestis* of Santa Maria, as well as Cida in the shelter for AIDS patients in Brasília – all of whom are people at the margins of society – search for a vocabulary in which their desires can be expressed, and which will provide them with signs to represent their differences. In the religious experience, *travestis* involve themselves in myths that allow them to expand their universe of belief and of interpretation, and in rituals that intensify and diversify their individual experiences.

As I see it, we would better understand the characters in this story if we were to think of them as people accessing sophisticated mythical apparatuses; as bodies injected with silicone and hormones that execute beautiful performances in *Quimbanda* rituals; as subjects in transit who use religious codices in order to reflect on their options and desires, or who perambulate spaces searching for their aspirations. In the framework that I have described in this chapter, there is no way to apply a proposal like Preciado's. This is not only because biopower is an open phenomenon that must be mapped (this includes its many varieties, such as the *pharmaco-pornopower* that Preciado suggests), but also because there are many diverse bodies in question. After all, the mediators here are different, and biotechnology mixes with entities and gods that conform to other bodies. Additionally, the form of acting (in other words, agency) is not the same in all contexts, nor is it independent from local histories.

We can therefore conclude that: (1) The *queer* political gesture seems to be distinct from the agency of Afro-Brazilian religious practitioners; (2) The *travestis* of

Santa Maria search for new grammars with which to express themselves; (3) There is no way of thinking about these bodies as removed from the intricate contexts that produced them; (4) There is also no way to simply apply theories formulated in other places, because the forms of subjectification are different here; (5) To decontextualize these bodies and souls would be to practice a kind of epistemological violence that acts by taking away that which is most important for the subjects involved, scorning their inventions and their forms of acting. This leads us to return to the questions formulated at the beginning of this chapter regarding the potentiality and adequacy of *queerness* in the tropics.

Translating *Queer?*

The potency of *queer* theory, and its ability not to congeal into previous theories removed from local histories, will depend on its capacity to absorb these other experiences and to alter itself. The reticence regarding the term *queer* – which, as we have seen, is not easily translated – could then be mitigated. As I mentioned in the beginning of this chapter, some authors have commented that the term *queer*, in and of itself, signals a certain asymmetry, since it always evokes an English-speaking, Western context for the world. However, if *queer* theory is instead able to open itself to other experiences and forms of knowledge – experiences that signal the differences of bodies, forms of agency, mediators, and subjectivities – and to be affected by them, then the possibility exists that, instead of being an English-language term, instead of signaling a process of consubstantiated asymmetry within an overpowering Eurocentrism, the expression might stand for a resistance to simple translations.

Sedgwick investigated the etymology of the term: "The word 'queer' itself means across – it comes from the Indo-European root *-twerkw*, which also yields the German *quer* (transverse), Latin *torquere* (to twist), English *athwart*". (Sedgwick, 1993, p. viii) *Queer* could be translated into Portuguese as meaning "strange"; "ridiculous"; "eccentric"; "rare"; or "extraordinary" (Sedgwik, 1993, p. xii); the expression is also used as a pejorative to designate dissident bodies (Louro, 2001). Various proposals have been made for translating *queer* theory into Portuguese: "*rarita* (weird) theory", "*transviado* (faggot) studies", or "slut theory". The discomfort that English-language terminology presents is notorious. These difficulties of translation remind me of a very beautiful text of Derrida (1985), in which he responds to a Japanese friend who wants to translate the term *deconstruction*. Derrida points out the impossibility of translating at the same time as he translates the expression "deconstruction", showing how the word might be substituted by another within the same language or between different languages (Ottoni 2005). In this attempt, Derrida shows how translators are involved with and compromised by the language they translate. He writes:

> The chance, first of all the chance of (the) "deconstruction", would be that another word (the same word and another) can be found in Japanese to say the same thing (the same and

another), to speak of deconstruction, and to lead elsewhere to its being written and transcribed, in a word which will also be more beautiful (Derrida 1985, p.5).

I propose here that more important than looking for direct equivalents for the term *queer* in one language or another is the necessity of "steering toward a new place", the necessity of "encounter" and "invention". In other words, steering toward translation as a transformation that implies involvement and commitment.

If, as some say, *queer* studies are paralyzed, it may be because they are petrified in the universal theories of the global North that are exported to the tropics in order simply to be applied, constituting a voyage of a certain geopolitics of knowledge that places some as "consumers" of *queerness* and others as "producers" of universal theories. And it is probable that any promise of rejuvenation might be linked to the possibilities of escaping from these traps through processes of distorting or dislocating theories. Thus, on this side of the equator, we must think of the affects and affectations that can dislocate these universalizing and far-removed theories toward local histories. *Queer* theory would then be affected and reconfigured in processes of translation brought about by these other-experiences. The term *queer*, in this case, signals a sempiternal movement in which the desire to translate serves as an opening toward the Other, discovering the potentials of mother tongues and thereby drawing out the horizons of different perspectives. Taking in this foreign term that is at once untranslatable and that requires translation may produce a reconfiguration of languages and perspectives within this unstable process of the construction of the comparable[13] (Ricoeur, 2006). *Queerness* will then force language to ballast itself to strangeness (from the term *estrangeiro* – foreigner – that resists, through "excentric" bodies and diverse practices), and these experiences in the tropics will invent an opening to new grammars and new forms of action, like the *travestis* "working their bodies" in the saints' houses of Santa Maria teach us.

References

Anzaldúa, G. (1999). *La frontera/borderlands*. London: Consortium Book Sales and Distribution.
Augras, M. (1989). De Yiá Mi a Pomba Gira: transformações e símbolos da libido, In: M. de C. E. Moura, org., *Meu sinal está no teu corpo: eséritos sobre a religião dos orixás*. São Paulo, Edicon/Edusp, 14–44.
Birman, P. (1985). Identidade social e homossexualismo no candomblé. *Religião & Sociedade*, Rio de Janeiro, 12(1), pp.2–21.
Birman, P. (1995). *Fazer estilo criando gêneros: possessão e diferenças de gênero em terreiros de umbanda e candomblé no Rio de Janeiro*. Rio de Janeiro: Relume Dumará.
Birman, P. (2005). Transas e transes: sexo e gênero nos cultos afro brasileiros – um sobrevôo. *Estudos Feministas, 13*(2), 403–414.
Braga, R. G. (1998). *Batuque Jêje-Ijexá em Porto Alegre: a música no culto aos orixás*. Porto Alegre: Fumproarte/Secretaria Municipal da Cultura de Porto Alegre.

---

[13] This is a comparison that seeks to exceed its own conceptual vocabulary, opening itself to others (Scott 2007), avoiding producing a monolithic notion of a cultural Other anchored in exoticism, and that works at registering colonial traditions (Butler 2007).

Butler, J. (1990). *Gender trouble: Feminism and the subversion of identity*. New York: Routledge.

Butler, J. (2005). *Giving an account of oneself*. New York: Fordham University Press.

Butler, J. (2007). Pour ne pas en finir avec le 'Genre'... Table ronde. *Sociétés et Représentations, 2*(24), 285–306.

Cabral, M. (2009). Salvar las distancias: apuntes acerca de "biopolíticas del género". In *Biopolítica* (pp. 123–138). Buenos Aires: Ají de Pollo.

de Carvalho, J. J. (1990). Xangô. In *Sinais dos tempos: diversidade religiosa no Brasil* (pp. 131–138). Rio de Janeiro: Instituto de estudos da Religião.

de Carvalho, J.J. (1994). Violência e caos na experiência religiosa. A dimensão dionisíaca dos cultos afro-brasileiros. In: C.E.M. Moura, org., *As senhoras do pássaro da noite*. São Paulo: Edusp.

Connell, R. (2010). *Southern theory: The global dynamics of knowledge in social science*. Cambridge: Polity Press.

Conner, R., & Sparks, H. (2004). *Queering creole spiritual traditions: Lesbian, Gay, Bisexual, and transgender participation in African-Inspired traditions in the Americas*. New York/London/Oxford: Harrington Park Press.

Contins, M., & Goldman, M. (1984). O caso da pombagira. Religião e violência: uma análise do jogo discursivo entre umbanda e sociedade. *Religião e Sociedade, 11*(1), 103–132.

Corrêa, N. (1992). *O batuque do Rio Grande do Sul. Antropologia de uma religião afro-rio-grandense*. Porto Alegre: UFRGS.

Correa, N. (1994). Panorama das religiões afro-brasileiras do Rio Grande do Sul. In A. P. Oro (Ed.), *As religiões afro-brasileiras do Rio Grande do Sul* (pp. 9–46). Porto Alegre: UFRGS.

Das, V. (2007). *Life and words: Violence and the descent into the ordinary*. Berkeley: University of California Press.

De Lauretis, T. (1991). Queer theory: Lesbian and gay sexuality – An introduction. *Differences: Journal of Feminist Cultural Studies, 3*(2), iii–xviii.

Derrida, J. (1985). Letter to a Japanese Friend. (Prof. Izutsu). In Wood & Bernasconi (Eds.), *Derrida and Differance* (pp. 1–5). Warwick: Parousia Press.

Fischer, A.E. (2009). Des dudas, dialogo y preguntas sobre Agnes biodrag y una insurrección de saberes. *Biopolítica*. Buenos Aires: Ají de Pollo, pp.107–118.

Foucault, M. (1978). *The will to knowledge: The history of sexuality* (Vol. 1). New York: Radom House.

Fry, P. (1977). Mediunidade e sexualidade. *Religião e Sociedade, 1*, 105–123.

Fry, P. (1982). Homossexualidade masculina e cultos afro-brasileiros. In: P. Fry, org., *Para inglês ver*. Rio de Janeiro: Zahar. 54–73.

Goldman, M. (2009). Histórias, devires e fetiches das religiões afro-brasileiras: ensaio de simetrização antropológica. *Análise Social: Revista do Instituto de Ciências Sociais da Universidade de Lisboa, 190*, 105–137.

Heidegger, M. (1986). Batir habiter penser. In *Essais et conférences*. Paris: Gallimard.

Leão Teixeira, M.L. (2000b2000a). Lorogun: identidades sexuais e poder no candomblé. In: C.E.M. de Moura, org., *Candomblé: religião de corpo e alma*. São Paulo: Pallas. pp.33–52.

Louro, G. L. (2001). Teoria Queer: uma política pós-identitária para a educação. *Estudos Feministas, 9*(2).

Meyer, M. (1993). *Maria Padilha e toda sua quadrilha: de amante de um rei de Castela a pombagira de umbanda*. São Paulo: Duas Cidades.

Miskolci, R. (2009). A teoria queer e a sociologia: o desafio de uma analítica da normalização. *Sociologias, 21*, 150–182.

Motta, R. (1995). Sacrifício, mesa, festa e transe na religião afro-brasileira. *Horizontes Antropológicos, 1*(3), 31–38.

Muñoz, J. E. (1999). *Disidentifications: Queers of color and the performance of politics*. Minneapolis: University of Minnesota Press.

Muñoz, J. E. (2006). Feeling Brown, feeling down: Latina affect, the performativity of race, and the depressive position. *Signs: Journal of Women and Culture and Society, 31*(3), 675–688.

Oro, A.P. org. (1994). *As religiões afro-brasileiras do Rio Grande do Sul*. Porto Alegre: UFRGS.

Oro, A. P. (2002). Religiões afro-brasileiras do Rio Grande do Sul: passado e presente. *Estudos afro-asiáticos, 24*(2), 345–384.

Oro, A. P. (2008). As religiões afro-brasileiras do Rio Grande do Sul. *Debates do NER, Porto Alegre, 9*(13), 9–23.

Oro, A. P. (2012). O atual campo afro-religioso gaúcho. *Civitas: revista de ciências sociais., 12*(3), 556–565.

Ottoni, P. (2005). Introdução. In: P. Ottoni, org., *Tradução: a prática da diferença*. Campinas: Unicamp. 11–19.

Pereira, P. P. G. (2004). *O terror e a dádiva*. Goiânia: Cânone.

Pereira, P. P. G. (2006). A teoria queer e a reinvenção do corpo. *Cadernos Pagu, 27*, 469–477.

Pereira, P. P. G. (2013). In and around life: Biopolitics in the tropics. *Vibrant, 10*, 13–37.

Pereira, P. P. G. (2014). *De corpos e travessias. Uma antropologia de corpos e afetos*. São Paulo: Annablume.

Prandi, R. (1996). *Pomba-gira dos candomblés e as faces inconfessas do Brasil. Herdeiras do Axé* (pp. 139–164). São Paulo: Hucitec.

Preciado, P. B. (2002a). *Manifiesto contra-sexual: prácticas subversivas de identidad sexual*. Madrid: Pensamiento Opera Prima.

Preciado, P. B. (2002b). *Basura y Género, Mear/Cagar. Masculino/Femenino*. Bilbao: Amasté.

Preciado, P. B. (2008). *Testo Yonqui*. Madrid: Espasa.

Preciado, P. B. (2009). La invención del género, o el tecnocordero que devora a los lobos. In *Biopolítica* (pp. 15–42). Buenos Aires: Ají de Pollo.

Rich, A. (1993). Compulsory heterosexuality and lesbian existence. In H. Abelove, M. A. Barale, & D. M. Halperin (Eds.),. Orgs. *The lesbian studies and gay studies*. New York: Routledge.

Ricoeur, P. (2006). *On Translation*. London/New York: Routledge.

Rose, N. (2007). *The politics of life itself: Biomedicine, power, and subjectivity in the twenty-first century*. Princeton: Princeton University Press.

San Martín, F. R. (2009). Biopolítica, tecnología en red y subversión. In *Biopolítica* (pp. 75–102). Buenos Aires: Ají de Pollo.

Santos, M. S. (2008). Sexo, gênero e homossexualidade: o que diz o povo-de-santo paulista? *Horizonte, 6*(12), 145–156.

Scott, J. W. (2007). Pour ne pas en finir avec le 'Genre'…, Round table with Judith Butler, Éric Fassin and Joan Wallach Scott. *Sociétés et Représentations, 24*, 285–306.

Sedgwick, E. K. (1993). *Tendencies*. Durham and London: Duke University Press.

Segato, R. L. (1995). *Santos e daimonis: O politeísmo afro-brasileiro e a tradição arquetipal*. Brasília: UnB.

Trindade, L. (1985). *Exu, poder e perigo*. São Paulo: Ícone.

Chapter 4
Decolonial Queer

Queer theory emerged as a critique of the normalizing effects of identity formation, and as a possible means of grouping dissident bodies. It is a theory that delineates transgressive interventions and possibilities beyond binary construction of the sexes, and that rethinks ontologies; a theory that opposes itself to the hetero epistemologies that dominate scientific production. In multiple journeys, and in intense movements of theories and people, queer theory encounters decolonial thinking, which is a critical perspective on the "coloniality of power"; in other words, a conceptual, political, ethical, and productive construct of the social spheres forged in Europe during the early centuries of colonization (Quijano 1991, 1998, 2000). By seeking out a counter position to the various logics of coloniality, and by presenting other cultural, political, and economic experiences and productions of knowledge, decolonial thinking alerts us to a certain direction in the voyages of theories, and to a geopolitics that transforms certain people into suppliers of experiences, and others into exporters of theories to be applied and reaffirmed.

This chapter accompanies these voyages of theories, through the Spanish and Portuguese speaking world, with the aim of *delineating* the principal outlines of the encounter between queer theory and decolonial thinking. As we know, delineating carries with it a sense of designing, sketching, delimiting, and tracing, but also a sense of conceiving and of planning (in an architectural context). Thus, the movement here is both a description and proposition ("proposition", in this case, meaning both presenting and proposing) of a *decolonial queer* form of thinking. In a preliminary way, the chapter formulates questions such as: could this encounter between decolonial thinking and queer theory produce something that might be thought of as "decolonial queer theory" (as enunciated in this chapter's title)? Or are these theories incompatible, given that the term *queer*, rendered in English, signals the very sort of geopolitics that decolonial thinking attempts to counter? Is there any commonality between these proposals? What is the potential of this encounter, and what might it produce? And what sorts of movements would a queer decolonial reading design?

P. P. G. Pereira, *Queer in the Tropics*, SpringerBriefs in Sociology,
https://doi.org/10.1007/978-3-030-15074-7_4

Of Theories and Voyages

When queer theory travels through the Spanish and Portuguese speaking world, it becomes a crooked theory, a theory of the asshole, a faggot theory, a twisted theory, a pink theory, a transgressive theory that questions, critically, the very position of theory and its supposedly immaculate character (Bento 2014; Córdoba 2007; Guasch 1998; Jiménez 2002; Pelúcio 2014b). Thereby, at least here in the Global South, this movement serves as an alert against the aspirations of a "universal" (Eurocentric, white, and hetero) theory that aspires to embrace everything (Miskolci 2014a).

It is important to emphasize, however that here in the Global South, Queer Theory arose and came into being as an open term that allowed us to confront the hegemony of the Global North in producing and disseminating social theories, as well as to its pressure in creating disciplines. The term "Queer Theory", as originally used in the United States, may refer to a critical and counter-normal gaze that served as a common denominator for a vast and diverse cross-section of academic production. But it was not only in the United States that people connected to gender and sexuality studies sought the works of Deleuze, Derrida, Foucault, Kristeva, and Wittig – among others – to create a counter-discourse, as authors like Richard Miskolci have observed (Miskolci 2014b, p. 12). Here in the tropics, we have reinvented and reconstructed queer genealogy, extending it to new areas, thereby amplifying and modifying what Queer Theory is understood to be in a North American context. This modification has taken place to such an extent that, here in the tropics, queer theory has virtually raised the possibility of distancing itself from, as I affirmed above, pretensions of universality (Miskolci and Pelúcio 2007).

This movement implies a conscious abdication of authority, and it insinuates itself as impure and improbable. To such an extent that, here in the Global South, queer theory arose narrowly linked to the interpellation of multitudes of dissident bodies, that calls itself into question, and that takes seriously the risk of transforming itself (Sharon 2005). This is because the term that qualifies it could be abandoned in favor of others that produce more efficient political actions (Butler 1998).

The proliferation of new languages produces the sentiment of discomfort and incompleteness, of malleability, and of the necessity of living through translations. This type of frequent experience exposes queer theory to affectations that produce changes and transformations. In conforming to the means of affectations and affects of dissident bodies, queer theory in the Global South can only imagine itself through the process of a permanent decolonization. It is therefore a theory stretched to its own limits, that jokes at its own expense and fluctuates with the interpellations of bodies, and that – between this shaking up and outright abdication, tends to fall in love with other theories: specifically, with the other-theories that emerge from the multiplicity of bodies and subjectivities. In sum, my argument here is that Queer Theory is an agonistic theory that sees its only possibility for existing in the practice of distancing itself from itself in order, paradoxically, to construct itself as possibility.

However, what is *queer* is not beyond the differences of power and prestige in the itineraries of theories. Regardless of its subversive potential queer theory is inserted into a geopolitical context. When queer theory travels to the Global South, it carries with it the challenges, dangers, and potentialities that all voyages present. Here, there is a temptation to simply apply queer theory as though the term "queer" and the subversion that it provokes (through the destabilization of theory itself) did not also act through dislocations. It is as though when queer theory travels its abdication of initial authority were forgotten; and as though that theory later reemerged, now in the position of theory ready to be applied.[1] According to Larissa Pelúcio, we have tended to receive queer knowledge by incorporating theories from the Global North without a due critique of imperialism (Pelúcio 2014b; Miskolci 2014b). In Pelúcio's terms, according to the anatomized geography of the world, the Global South's place would be in "the asshole of the world" (Pelúcio 2014a, p. 10). We went, below the equator, localizing ourselves in peripheral confines and, to a certain extent, we recognized this geography as legitimate. And, Pelúcio continues, if the world has an asshole, it also has a head; a thinking head, in its north. This morphological metaphor illustrates the geopolitics that I take on over the course of this chapter. But, applying queer theory – i.e., accepting in our space what was formulated far away – is a sort of escape from the field of queerness. In this case, it becomes a trick against queerness.

If this trick moves through its voyages to the Global South as an imminent presence, it need not pass through dangerous itineraries: this because voyages also subvert theories, producing something beyond a theory to be applied. This is also because voyages are complex forms of interweaving. Researchers from the Global South travel to the North and come face to face with queer theory. But queer theory does not only travel through people who come from the Global North; books and articles also travel to the Global South, which they crisscross in complex itineraries. Books and articles also travel, and their paths that do not always coincide with those travelled by paths.[2]

In the Global North, it finds multiple frameworks. For example, for almost a decade, Queer of Color Critique has been questioning the white and middle-class nature of the analyses that were first recognized as Queer Theory. There is also a re-discussion of queer genealogy that aims to recognize the Chicana feminist Gloria Anzaldúa as one of its creators (Miskolci 2014b, p. 13; Ochoa 2011). In the midst of the machine that reproduces canonical Theories, and the institutionalized departments (and disciplines) that are historically linked to white, heterosexual intellectual elites, these researchers opt to approximate themselves to formulations of dissident bodies. In queerness, they find a more open position in reaction to a certain normalized gay/lesbian gaze that has traditionally guided studies of sexuality, even in the Global South (Colling 2015; Miskolci 2014b). Queer theory's voyage to the Global South is also part of the actions of the researchers and activists who

---

[1] For an article analyzing how queer theory is produced, how it circulates, and how it is read in an Anglophone context, see Miskolci and Pelúcio (2017).

[2] See the concept of diasporic ethnography in Ochoa (2014).

appropriate this theory, creating noise and dissonance in response to the way things are done in this part of the world.

People walk, they travel, they pass through, and they move themselves. And their path, their itinerary, changes them, transforming them into something different at the provisional end of any given trajectory. This process acts on bodies that feel the effects of other languages, habits, and ways of being in the world, and these bodies become something different. This becoming is not totally controlled; such is the beauty of trajectories. Like bodies, theories also travel, and the transpositions that play out in unheard paths and encounters transform these theories into processes of dislocation, movement, and multiplicity. These transpositions, encounters, and voyages lead us on our search, which I alluded to in the beginning of this chapter, for interweaving theories. If queerness constructs itself in a conceptual movement that tends to open itself to other theories, how might it come to encounter decolonial thinking?[3]

The Encounter

When theories travel, they come face to face with a conceptual and political structure, and with an ethics of the management of social spheres forged in Europe in the early centuries of colonization, all of which Anibal Quijano refers to as "coloniality" (Quijano 1991, 1998, 2000). Quijano attempts to account for a context that draws out the history of colonialism at the same time as he reveals the continuity of colonial forms of domination even after colonial administrations officially ended. He shows how certain processes that originated or were accentuated with colonization are renewed, even as we are told that they have supposedly been overcome, assimilated, or become outmoded. Thus, colonialism and coloniality are different but related concepts: the first points to specific historical periods, whereas the second reveals the underlying logic of colonial undertakings as the colonial matrix of power.

This logic manifests itself in the transformation of cultural differences in values and hierarchies of geopolitics, race, and gender. Distinctions become epistemological and ontological classifications, and whoever controls classification controls knowledge. The process of transforming differences into values creates inferior zones. Colonial difference is a process of control, a strategy to demean certain populations and certain regions of the world. The concept of coloniality allows us to understand these classifications and hierarchies, suggesting that colonial difference is an accomplice to universalism, sexism, and racism.

To decolonize is to extricate ourselves from the logic of coloniality and its effects, and to detach ourselves from the apparatus that confers prestige and meaning to Europe. In other words, decolonization is an operation that consists of

---

[3] This passage was inspired by María Lugones's concept of world-travelling, as found in Lugones (1987).

detaching ourselves from Eurocentrism and, in the same movement with which we extricate ourselves from its logic and its apparatus, opening ourselves to other experiences, stories, and theories. It involves opening ourselves to Others that have been covered over by the logic of coloniality: those Others that have become lesser, abject, and disqualified.[4]

In opening ourselves to other logics, claiming the importance and magnitude of these other-thought, questioning Theories, and believing in a multitude of theories and bodies, decolonial thinking approximates that which we call queerness. Like queer theory, decolonial criticism interrogates the theoretical pretentions that generalize certain assumptions and subjects, and that elude the formulations of Others, which are considered to be specific and particular. Confident in this approximation, several authors have worked at constructing encounters between queer and decolonial thinking.[5] It is certainly true that the outlines of this approximation are still cloudy, and that the path has yet to be fully laid. At present, there is a strong necessity for consolidating the encounter between queer theory and decolonial theorists that elaborate critiques of coloniality starting from Latin America and the Caribbean.[6] Tracing this path is certainly still a task to be carried out, in spite of the many praiseworthy efforts and initiatives that this chapter seeks to join.

Given this variety of theoretical options and persistent lacunas, it is not strange that, in the relations between queer theory and decolonial thinking, many current formulations appear to be suspect. Queerness – embraced by a multitude of "strange" bodies – travels, placing itself before those who suspect certain voyages of theories, such as decolonial thinking. This suspicion is based on the alleged proximity of *queer* theory to theories formulated in the Global North. The very term *queer* is exceedingly difficult to translate, which means that even as it travels to diverse places, it preserves itself it English, thereby signaling a geopolitics of knowledge that decolonial thinking seeks to oppose. Thus, problems of literal translation become superimposed in terms of conflicts regarding the production of knowledge along a North-South axis.[7] For its part, queer theory also tends to be suspicious of the use of reified identities, and of theoretical proposals that are not attuned to questions of the body. It also is suspicious of the geopolitical framing that forgets its origins as an nonconforming way of thinking about nonconforming bodies. From its beginnings, queer theory has taken pride in what was once an insult attributed to segments considered to be abject or lacking in prestige.

---

[4] I have been very inspired by a number of different decolonial authors. As it is impossible to cite them all, I will name the following: Castro-Gomez (2007); Mignolo (2000, 2008); Segato (2013, 2014); Walsh (2004, 2009).

[5] Examples include: Canfield (2009); Hawley (2001); Perez (2003). Approximations between feminism and decolonial criticism can be found in the work of Lugones (2005, 2007, 2011, 2012). For an analysis of the difference between post-colonial and decolonial thinking, see Grosfoguel (2006).

[6] About elaborate critiques of coloniality starting from Latin America and the Caribbean, see Mignolo (1998).

[7] On the question of translation, see Lugarinho (2001); Pelúcio (2014a); Rivas (2011); Sancho (2014). To accompany an analysis of translation and the travels of theories, see Möser (2013).

In spite of these suspicions, there are also, as I mentioned earlier, approximations between queer theory and decolonial thinking. In its search to reveal the underlying logic of colonial undertakings, decolonial thinking seeks to reveal how constructions of gender and sexuality overlap in or are the products of colonialization (Lugones 2007, 2011, 2012; Segato 2012, 2013). If the Canon is Eurocentric, hetero, and white, queerness jokes with these places and Theories, and with their presumed universality. It also calls their heteronormativity into question. Decolonial thinking denounces the processes of construction at work in this universality, and it suspects these Theories, demonstrating how the "colonial wound" expands and takes on the imposition of a sex-gender system as an ontological determination that installs itself in European colonies (Maldonado-Torres 2007; Suriaga 2011). Meanwhile, queer theory makes possible a critique of history's gazes as being refracted through a heteronormative lens, interpreting the configuration of sex and gender as part of the colonial project. Queer theory and decolonial thinking open themselves to and believe in Other bodies, histories, and theories.

Presumably, both queer theory (here, I am referring to the queer theory that is being produced and reinvented in the Global South) and decolonial thinking ought to refute the tendency of travelling theories in which the Global South supplies data and experiences for the Global North to theorize and transform into further exportable theories (Connell 2010).

Queer theory and decolonial thinking either abdicate from or subvert conceptual machinery that defines itself as universal and necessarily applicable; both emerge from a place of contempt, ridiculing or denouncing Theory and its pretentious universal applicability. In reality, both queer theory and decolonial criticism must be affected by bodies and experiences, which leads to their propensity to become caught up in the dilemmas of processes of translation. The term "queer" does not have a direct translation in either Portuguese or Spanish, so when it arrived in these parts, queerness already carried within it a necessity for translation, as though the very difficulty of translating the term *queer* served as a telos for the seemingly impossible; in other words, for translation itself. Decolonial thinking also asserts the potency of other-theories, such as those of dissident and radicalized bodies. Some authors, for example, mention the construction of a "pluritopic hermeneutics" with an intuition for perceiving the conflicts that originate in collisions of cosmovisions, while still recognizing and rescuing preserving other traditions and ways of thinking (Mignolo 2000).

Thus, queer theory and decolonial thinking configure themselves as open areas of study, and they are defined exactly to the extent that they affect and are affected by Others. What makes the encounter between these theories probable and fecund is that they are not modes of thinking closed in upon themselves, but rather opening movements for Others, movements of insertion in other-theories and in other forms of thinking and being.

Queer theory and decolonial thinking are fields in construction, spaces of confluence between the forces of bodies and of geopolitics. They are expressions of colonial difference as manifest in bodies. These bodies are not simply time-bodies, but also space-bodies: they are bodies that are inveterate in certain spaces (Mignolo 2008).

Queer bodies are constituted according to colonial difference. There is no way of separating abject bodies and dissident sexuality from geographic location, from language, from history, and from culture. Queer theory is also a politics of localization: both queer theory and decolonial thinking are embodied theories.

Neither queer theory nor decolonial thinking profess a simple rejection of theories from the Global North: instead, they are *ideas and practices*, embodied and localized, that denounce these geopolitical divisions and call them into question, moving themselves in such a way as to both *break with* and *recuperate* theories (rupture and recovering, as I mentioned in the chapter *In and around life*) thereby producing something new (Stoler 1995). But – returning to a question to which I have already alluded – what movements might a decolonial queer reading design? And what potency would such movements have in identifying colonial machinery's capacity to act in reading concepts that travel, with all of its silences and obliterations?

Concepts and Their Voyages

Pierre Bourdieu, writing about the circulation of ideas and the types of voyages to which I have referred here, highlights a short passage written by Karl Marx in the *Communist Manifesto* about texts circulating outside of their original context (Bourdieu 2002). Marx observes that German thinkers have a poor understanding of French thinkers because they receive French texts – which are impregnated with political conjunctures – as pure texts. Thereafter, Marx notes, German thinkers transform the political agent that was present from the beginning into a transcendental subject. This is one aspect of the circulation of ideas, in all its dissonance. But there are still other problems in the voyages of theories, and perhaps a meaningful issue might be – as I have tried to formulate here – the fact that authors from "central" countries export concepts and theories that, later, are applied independently of local histories. This takes place to such an extent that, in the Global South, there is always the possibility of applying and replicating a theory that was not only unique to other contexts, but that was also forged in a process of obliterating the experiences of local histories. In order to think about this type of voyage and about the transit of ideas and theories, a good example might be the Italian philosopher Giorgio Agamben.

Agamben's influence and presence may be due to the scope of his undertaking, given that he has dedicated himself to understanding the political life of the West, and to formulating a critique of Western metaphysics. In terms of understanding political life, Agamben avails himself of four central and interwoven concepts: sovereign power; bare life *(homo sacer)*; the state of exception; and the concentration camp (Agamben 1998, 2002, 2004a, 2004b, 2005, 2006 – see chapter *In and aroud life*). According to Agamben, these concepts permeate Western politics, and reach their maximum saturation in modernity.

To elucidate how states of exception were brought into being in Republics and Constitutional States, Agamben analyzes the history of governments, passing from the Roman Senate to the French Revolution, through both World Wars, and up to the events of September 11, 2001. However, Agamben's sophisticated, erudite, and historically extensive analysis of the origin and development of political and legal thought in the West stands in stark contrast to his profound silence regarding the history of colonization. Throughout his work, Agamben makes only fleeting references to colonization, without stopping to examine concrete histories.[8] In his attempt to understand the political life of the West, Agamben never explores the modes through which the geopolitical entity known as "The West" emerges through the domination of Others. In reality, Agamben elaborates his theoretical outline (with concepts such as *homo sacer*; fields; sovereignty; and state of exception) without references to colonialism, or to critical interventions of struggles against colonial oppression and against the imperial logic of control based on racial exclusion. His body of work does not stop to examine specific histories or concrete social circumstances of the present state of exception, of the relations of abandonment in colonial structures, or the relations between colony and empire (Shenhav 2012). This silence becomes even greater when we recall that Agamben developed his theoretical contributions in a post-colonial context. Moreover, there is a relevant body of literature of post-colonial authors, such as Edward Said, Gayatri Spivak, and Homi Bhaba, as well as the previously-cited theory of coloniality of the Global North: one of the few theories to go against the grain of the geopolitics that divides the world between North and South (Segato 2013).

How, therefore, can we explain how an erudite thinker with vast historical knowledge might obliterate a significant part of the history that produced the concepts fundamental to his theoretical output? The possible response to this inquiry would lead us to localize Agamben's work as being immersed in a Eurocentrism that universalizes provincial theories (Chakrabarty 2000), and that limits its potential and capacity for perception to the horizon of the Western political tradition (Kalyvas 2005). In this same sense, the silences and silencing(s) of Agamben's output can be contextualized in the context of coloniality: his theories are impregnated by the apparatus and the logic that construct and reproduce Eurocentrism. When Agamben forgets certain historical experiences, it is due to the actions of an apparatus that defines Europe as both the primary model and as the *de facto* center.

In spite of this provincial character, we can *recuperate* concepts such as *homo sacer* and of the state of exception in order to aid our comprehension of the reality of colonization, and of the politics of exclusion and abandonment that are so characteristic of the colonial situation. Agamben examines how the state of exception has become a permanent paradigm in Western democracies. As previously mentioned, he explores the European genealogy of exception that articulates the

---

[8]Agamben (2002, 2006) makes oblique mentions of colonization and of colonial prison camps, specifically in regards to the Spanish colonization of Cuba and the British colonization of South Africa (Shenhav 2012). Beyond this, in his essay *Metropolis*, he examines the tropes of colonial and post-colonial analysis (Svirsky and Bignall, 2012). But that is all.

relationship between law and exception – a relationship that is essential to the state's violent practices – but he does not confront the relationships between colonialism and imperialism that are so fundamental to understanding exception. This is especially true given that imperialism was the arena in which the state of exception was implemented most systematically and violently. At the beginning of the twentieth century, a time when European colonies occupied 85% of the world's territory, political spaces appeared in which imperial powers implemented alternative models of rules, making this context especially propitious for studies of sovereignty (Fieldhouse 1967). Colonialism is one of the best examples for any theoretical study of norms and exceptions, of the rule of law, and of emergencies, especially because emergency was used as an elastic category throughout Europe's colonies, varying in events such as insurgencies. For example, in Olivier Le Cour Grandmaison's analysis of the French colonial experience in Algeria, he demonstrates how judicial and military techniques of exception that developed in the colony were later used to suppress class revolts in European metropolises (Grandmaison 2005). Grandmaison concludes that any attempt to understand the "political matrix of power" through the logic of exception must necessarily consider the state of exception from a colonial perspective.

Bearing in mind Grandmaison's formulation, would it not also be interesting to investigate whether the colony might serve as a paradigm for modernization in place of (and more appropriately than) the "concentration camp" (Eaglestone 2002)? And might the colonial concept of law be more adequate for understanding the jurisprudence of emergency (Hussain 2003)? It would be interesting to recall, as demonstrated by Hannah Arendt, that concentration camps first appeared at the beginning of the twentieth century during the Boer Wars, a dispute between colonizing countries over diamond and gold mines in what we now know as South Africa (Arendt 1989). These camps remained active in South Africa and India as a form of dealing with undesirables. The expression "protective custody", later used by the Third Reich, emerged at this time. As we have noted, concentration camps, the jurisprudence of emergency, and *homo sacer* are all closely related to processes of colonization.

What, then, would a queer decolonial reading be? What movements might it design? Its efforts would seek to *break with* the apparatus and logic of coloniality, to signal them in its movements, and to move away from them, while perceiving Agamben's body of work – and its silence regarding colonial history – in the context of coloniality. This effort would also direct itself toward *altering* concepts, *transforming* them in such a way that they might produce something new, and apply more broadly and in different ways. In this case, Agamben's theory about the state of exception and biopolitics in the West would be situated within the history of colonial relations, a theoretical-conceptual movement that would allow us to identify the coloniality of power as a formative dimension in the West's political paradigm. This movement would be one of detachment, of breaking with Eurocentrism and its limits, and of inverting and modifying concepts, transforming them in such a way and with such intensity as to make them produce something new, making them speak more and in another way. And in order to say something more, it is worth interpellating beyond the politics of localization and the place of enunciation, and toward the corporality of these theories.

For example, Lentin (2006) explores specific forms of state-sanctioned violence based on her work with survivors' testimonies. The histories of women survivors lead her to ask whether the category of *homo sacer* has gendered implications, and whether there might be a female equivalent in "bare life." In other words, might a *femina sacra* exist? The author concludes that a woman, when at the mercy of sovereign power, exercises the function of vehicles for ethnic cleansing, thereby becoming *femina sacra*: someone who can be killed, but not sacrificed. Lentin follows the same directions as other analyses of feminicide, in which women's bodies become metaphors for nations and territories, and are placed at the center of disputes (Segato 2006, 2014).

Here in the Global South, various researchers have shown how colonial difference and the logic of coloniality act through a construction of what is human at the expense of women, Black people, and queer bodies (Mignolo 2006). Agamben's work, however, does not question or consider social actors' gender as part of life; Agamben does not consider the *homo sacer* within the dimension of gender or sexuality. There is also a disincarnation manifest in his analytic procedures: Agamben operates by erasing his corporeal connection as researcher, maintaining himself as separate from an incorporation susceptible to forcing or limiting him. From this disincarnated, de-localized position, Agamben places himself in opposition to women, to queer bodies, to radicalized bodies, all rooted in an non-transposable corporality.[9] What appears by default, then, is Agamben's masculine, Western, and white condition. He is a subject without depth, distanced from incarnate, incorporated subjects. He is distant because of his obliteration of his histories, because of his lack of attention to the colonial differences that produce sexualized and radicalized bodies.

This distance is constructed through analytic procedures that place themselves in opposition to the proposals of a decolonial queer way of thinking; that is to say, in opposition to the conjunction of corporeal and localized theories. Decolonial queer theory would therefore be a movement in search of eliminating this distance, a movement that wagers on other experiences, bodies, and ways of knowing. Agamben's movements in critiquing Western metaphysics reveal the difficulty of making such an analysis from within the West itself.[10] This difficulty speaks to the preeminent necessity of opening other theoretical movements: a propensity of decolonial queer theory through its investment in voyages, crossings, and paths that pass through the experiences of the bodies that travel them, trans-localize them, and derive from them, as well as in sophisticated forms of agencies.

---

[9] I am indebted here to the theoretical movements of Haraway (2007).

[10] This may be why Esposito (2010), the Italian philosopher, affirms: "I believe that a critical and self-critical image of the West can come to us only from outside the West, from a conceptual language that does not coincide with the West's own and whose specificity lies precisely in its difference from the West".

Other Movements

The intention of the previous section was clearly not to create an exegesis of Agamben's work. I merely aimed to emphasize the possibilities of queer decolonial readings, sketching out their embodied and localized theoretical movements. In point of fact, these movements – which, as I have said, I am both proposing and describing – are already prefigured in many different ways by multiple agents. For example, we can recall authors who have based their work, first and foremost, on post-colonial literature and subaltern studies (Hawley 2001); others who have been more influenced by migrants and their relations to the coloniality of the United States empire, such as those engaged with Chicanx Studies (Danielson 2009; Perez 2003; 2014; Soto 2010; Yarbro-Bejarano 1999); and authors who have interrogated social formations as intersections of race, gender, sexuality, and class, such as Queer People of Color Studies (Ferguson 2004; Johnson and Henderson 2005; Muñoz 1999, 2006). However, I would also like to highlight three contributions that I consider fundamental in thinking of a decolonial queer theory, especially because each of these examples has, in its own way, touched on the difficulty of critiquing western metaphysics from within the West.

The first contribution is that of María Lugones, who elaborates direct approximations between feminism and decolonial criticism (Lugones 1987, 2005, 2007, 2012). Lugones carries out a reading of the relationship between colonizer and colonized in terms of gender, race, and sexuality, proposing a rereading of capitalist modernity within modern coloniality. She shows how the colonial imposition of gender crosses through questions regarding ecology, economics, and government, as well as relating to the spiritual world and to knowledge in general. Lugones recalls that the Eurocentric colonial gender system produces non-humans, such as Black and indigenous women, who are neither represented by the universal category of "woman" or by the categories "Indian" and "Black". Lugones involves herself in Aymara social movements and cosmopolitics. In addition to presenting alternative ways of being in the world, Aymara concepts permit a critique of the hardening of modern configurations of gender, a critique of the coloniality of gender. Aymara cosmopolitics affect Lugones's thinking, an affectation that appears in her critique of the generalizations of feminist theories, and in her search to construct a decolonial feminism (Lugones 2011).

The second contribution is Mignolo (2007) who, for his part, presents Guaman Poma's decisive contribution to decolonial thinking. Poma was a Quechua and Aymara Indian who, writing in Spanish, produced a long critique regarding the harmful implications of Spanish colonization on Peru's indigenous communities. Writing in the sixteenth century, Guaman Poma proposes a form of government and management of the colony based on the perspective of the Inca Empire, framing imperial and Western history through both local systems of thought and knowledge and through colonial history. In Poma, Mignolo identifies the origin of the "paradigm of coexistence" that proposes an epistemological-spatial-temporal (geopolitical) rupture in articulating a Spanish-Indian-African triad. Through this paradigm,

Poma defended a horizontal form of organizing social institutions that ran counter to the imperial model of power. Mignolo argues that Poma's thinking was as important for Andean people as Marxism was for critical emancipatory thinking after the Industrial Revolution. Experiences and theories like Poma's allowed Mignolo to formulate the concept of "border thinking." In this sense, both Lugones and Mignolo open themselves to other cosmopolitics and other forms of knowledge, such as the saying that the decolonial option is a way of thinking that arises from the experience of exteriority, in the borders created by Europe's expansion within the world's diversity (Mignolo 2007).

The cosmopolitics and forms of knowledge that interpellate queer theory directly. This may be why one of the most important contributions in considering a decolonial queer theory is through indigenous queer studies. Within this already relatively extensive body of literature, the collection by Driskill et al. (2011) stands out. In it, the editors bring together critical approaches centered on indigenous populations in order to understand the lives and communities of gays, lesbians, transgender, queer, and Two-Spirit people (GLBTQ2). The book's objective is to provide inspiration for critical interventions in the re-imposition of native, queer, and indigenous studies. It is composed as a dialogue among a group of activist academics who revise the history of gay and lesbian studies in indigenous communities, and who simultaneously forge a path for indigenous theories and methodologies. Many of the essays deal with the possibilities of defining the LGBTQ2 acronym and delineating relations that sometimes cause queer theory to become fetishized. The book's organizers look into how old descriptions became substituted by decades of organization and writing by indigenous LGBTQ2 people. They also formulate insistent questions regarding how queer and indigenous theory informs their work, how the promotion of queer theory as "criticism without a subject" joins the efforts of indigenous studies in centralizing indigenous forms of knowledge and in carrying out a critical investigation of colonialism (Driskill et al. 2011, p. 2).[11] The Cherokee theoretician and activist Qwo-Li Driskill argues:

> David Eng, Judith Halberstam, and Muñoz have asked, "What does queer studies have to say about empire, globalization, neoliberalism, sovereignty, and terrorism? What does queer studies tell us about immigration, citizenship, prisons, welfare, mourning, and human rights?" While these moves in queer studies are creating productive theories, they haven't addressed the complicated colonial realities of Native people in the United States and Canada. In an attempt to answer the questions posited above within specifically Native contexts, Two-Spirit critiques point to queer studies's responsibility to examine ongoing colonialism, genocide, survival, and resistance of Native nations and peoples (Driskill 2010, p. 86).

These analyses emphasize the relationship between colonialism and sexuality, as well as the link between colonial development and heterosexuality. Anchored in erudite indigenous epistemologies and methodologies, the authors propose a remodeling of native studies, queer studies, transgender studies, and of indigenous

---

[11] To accompany how indigenous queer theorists have affected work relating to indigenous sexuality in Brazil, see Fernandes and Arisi (2017).

feminisms. The logic behind coloniality must be exposed, showing how constructions of gender and sexuality intersect and are products of colonialisms, framing the modern configuration of sex/gender as part of the colonial project. Decolonizing implies queering (see, for example, Smith 2010). The effect of indigenous queer critiques is so significant that currently, in the United States, it is not viable to study decolonial studies without approaching forms colonization that are currently in progress and indigenous/native modes of surviving.

Approaching from the same direction as these theoretical movements (and affected by these theoretical movements), I have also come across powerful other-theories here in the Global South. In Afro-Indigenous religious traditions, I have seen that the modern configuration of masculine-feminine does not coincide with the fluidity of sexual orientation and a model of sexuality marked by a transitivity of genders beyond that which colonialist culture represents, without tying gender to sexuality. I have perceived that decolonial queer theory passes through other histories and through sophisticated other-theories of sexuality and the body, as we will see below.

Other-Theories

Speaking of voyages, someone travelling by bus to the city of Santa Maria, in the state of Rio Grande do Sul, Brazil, might, if they are lucky, encounter Cilene – a beautiful *travesti* — at the bus station where she works as a custodian. From 2011 to 2015, I carried out research with Martha Souza regarding the itineraries of *travestis* in the Public Health System [Sistema Único de Saúde (SUS)] of Santa Maria, a city in the southern Brazilian state of Rio Grande do Sul. It did not take us long to find a gap in assistance that demonstrated the inadequacies of health services in attending to *travestis*. It was in this context that we met Cilene. In addition to interviews, conversations, and shared correspondence, Cilene insisted on writing her own story. Cilene's story tells us something about these dissident bodies, as well as about the possibilities of transit.

Born into a very poor family, Cilene was forced to leave school at a young age. Her departure was hastened by the everyday violence to which her classmates subjected her, as an "effeminate boy," as well as by the sexual abuse that she suffered at the hands of a school psychologist. Cilene's physical transformation was also very difficult: her family did not accept her, and she suffered frequent condemnations and punishments, especially from her father. In the midst of these conflicted relationships, which she did not know how to resolve, she had no option other than to leave home to "live with other *travestis*". However, she later tried to return to her family's home to care for her mother, who was "in poor health".

Cilene attempted to return to her family for years, but the same conflicts and her family's continued repudiation of her nonconforming body never allowed her. Her siblings believed that Cilene was a "freak", and her father completely rejected her, calling her "disgusting", and saying that any contact would be impossible. Her body, which she insisted was "beautiful and desired on the street", was "freakish" to her family.

According to Cilene, her "street life" was not very different from that of the other *travestis* in Santa Maria with whom she lived: she was surrounded constantly by beatings, fights, drugs, alcohol, injuries, scars, robberies, and investigations by the police, as well as insistent pressures from the "bosses of the block". Yet her street life was also a space for seeking support networks, especially among Santa Maria's other *travestis*. Cilene used hormones, which she injected on the same street corner where she "made the rent"; she eventually got silicone implants in her breasts with a locally known *bombadeira* (An amateur cosmetic surgeon; literally, a "pumper"). She still bears scars from this procedure which she calls her "whip marks," as though these scars were also part of constructing her body. Because of health problems, she stopped "working the streets" in 2010.

Decades passed until Cilene – patiently, and by taking advantage of "time's work" (Das 2007) – was once again able to live with her mother, siblings, and nieces and nephews. It was only after her father began to suffer from a debilitating illness that Cilene was able to return to her family home, this time protecting the man who had imposed a regime of violence on her, and caring for someone who had avoided all contact with her. Despite the fact that everyone in the house persisted in calling her by the masculine name with which she had been baptized, and the persistent conflicts that existed within the house, she found living with her family to be possible after her father's illness.

When Cilene describes her life, she highlights her love life and her family. Her narratives of her experiences focus on her romantic adventures as a girl. Based on her dissident body and her tenacity in claiming her ability to transform it according to her desires, Cilene weaves together her worries about her romances with concerns about her mother's health, as well as with her capacity for forgiveness, her cooking and cleaning, and the necessity of having patience. Aside from her discourse insisting on her rights, Cilene also presents an obstinate everydayness.

Cilene's insistence on maintaining romances and familial relations, on living in the everyday, and on recognizing on the importance of waiting highlights the agency of certain social actors who do not fit into typical notions of "agency". Usually, notions such as patience and passion are more closely linked to passivity than to resistance. Cilene's "descent into the everyday", however, shakes up pre-established models of resistance; or rather, it presents other possible forms of conceiving of these models. Different forms of dealing with exclusions and with the processes of becoming an abject figure exist, and many of these forms distance themselves from heroic models of resistance. Cilene also constructs a daily practice of transformation: her agency is not found in heroism and in the *extra-ordinary*, but rather in her descent into the everyday, in her daily preparations of meals, her cleaning, and her organization of chores, as well as in her persistent care for and cultivation of her familial relations.

If the expression *queer* is a proud form of manifesting difference, inasmuch as it can cause inversions in the chain of repetition that confers power to preexisting authoritarian practices, there is something new in Cilene's forms of action. By means of another grammar, Cilene expresses the discomforting and non-assimilable differences of bodies and souls that dare to make themselves present. Cilene goes out to the streets and participates in LGBT parades and in political actions that highlight her pride in being a *travesti*. She reenacts the queer act of facing injury, and of turning injury into something positive. This, however, is only one part of her agency. Cilene also overlooks her family's insults of "freak" and creates spaces of co-existence, allowing the passage of time and the process of waiting to make these offenses obviously inappropriate. This transformation takes place within a game of affectations and affects that reinvent forms of resistance. Here, another type of agency exists (Mahmood 2001).

Cilene's narrative signals a powerful theory of dealing with this tangle of loves and desires, and of waiting and patience:

> I'm a daughter of Oxum, the *orixá* of fresh water, of health, of beauty, and of fertility. My body belongs to Xapanã, the *orixá* of brooms, who sweeps negative and bad things far away, and who brings us good things with his seven brooms. All I have do to is ask Him.

By calling on Oxum to construct and give meaning to her female characteristics and her desire to "be part of the family", and on Xapanã to aid in her insistent quest to solve other peoples' problems, Cilene proposes other-theories in order to explain her descent into the everyday. Her body belongs to Xapanã, the *orixá* of smallpox and of all other skin diseases, who is responsible for causing illnesses, but also for curing them. This alignment, which I cannot by any means claim to approach here with the care that it deserves, signals an other-body that is different, produced by other mediations, and that is both shaped by and conforms to other subjectivities. These are bodies that are transformed by hormones and silicone, but that are also "worked through with the drum beats" of Afro-Brazilian religion.

In the last 2 years, since returning to her mother's house, Cilene has worked as an employee of the Santa Maria bus station, cleaning both the men's' and women's' bathrooms. This possibility is justified by the myth in which "Xapanã is the *orixá* of the broom, who sweeps negative and bad things far away". In the Santa Maria bus station, Cilene shuffles the terms "man" and "woman", and anchors her femininity in Oxum, and her agency in Xapanã. She inhabits a space of ambiguity in her everyday existence. This apparently ambiguous body cares for the apparatus (the bathroom) that acts by omitting ambiguity.

Public bathrooms are institutions that the bourgeoisie brought into being, and that became generalized in Europe during the nineteenth century (Preciado 2002). Though initially conceived of as spaces for managing human waste, they became, during the twentieth century, watchtowers for gender. They serve bodies recognized as fitting exclusively into a dualistic logic: "man and woman", and "masculine and feminine" become the defining adjectives for the physical space of the bathroom, and they configure these spaces, defining specific architectural forms for each gender. As Preciado demonstrates, bathrooms evaluate the degree to which bodies adhere to the standardized norms of masculinity and femininity.

Cilene is the person who takes care of the bathrooms in the Santa Maria bus station. When asked whether she herself uses the men's or women's room, she doesn't hesitate to answer: "The women's, of course!" However, she still transits between both spaces. The company she works for had to conduct a "juridical study" to avoid any "problems": in this sense, sweeping and washing latrines can also open the doors of the law.

As she focuses on family, on caring, and on her loves, Cilene's narratives are always accompanied by religious and philosophical incursions about the relation between myth and agency. Cilene accesses an Afro-Brazilian codex in order to situate herself within the world[12]; she also creates conditions in which she is able to wait for decades in order to live in her "family's house", as though this codex and these conditions were necessary in order to face the sobriquet "freak".

Cilene exists in the apparatuses that produce "normal", "hetero", and "non-ambiguous" bodies. Between the bathrooms in the bus station in the middle of the state of Rio Grande do Sul, she is referred to as Cilene – her "social name" – which is a conquest that she has yet to attain in her own home. Transiting between the fields of masculine and feminine, she signals that the architecture of bathrooms cannot encompass everyone. In this case, the apparatus for constructing genders is cared for by someone whose very existence highlights the failings of this apparatus and signals toward what can never be fully reached.

Cilene's story addresses us in a number of different ways, perhaps the most scathing of which is the form in which it makes our vocabulary obsolete: terms like "culture", "nature", "tradition", and "modernity" seem to lose their habitual meanings. A modified body (modified both through sophisticated technologies and by back-alley *bombadeiras*) belonging to a girl from the interior of Brazil; the management of sophisticated forms of knowledge; and the construction of a grammar of gender and sexuality that removes itself from compulsory heterosexuality: these are bodies that reinvent biology.

The obsolescence of vocabulary challenges us to think about theories. As we have seen, Cilene speaks about agency and deals with abjection in different ways than those we are accustomed to reading about in either queer theory or decolonial thinking. In addition, Cilene's experiences show us that the construction of a dissident body is not the same everywhere, and that this construction is also situated through other mediators and other bodies. Finally, Cilene presents another form of describing the world, a movement through which she shows that, beyond problems of representation, there are worlds that can vary and that cannot be reduced to the Global North's canons of rationality.[13]

Faced with this interpellation, perhaps our central inquiry is not to show how Cilene's story corroborates a decolonial criticism, or to signal it as part of queer theory, but rather to explore how these other-theories affect (in the strongest sense

---

[12] Segato (1998) defines the Afro-Brazilian religious codex as the grouping of repeated and embodied themes and motives in the interaction between divinities in this pantheon. These themes and motives can also be found in patterns of social interaction, in ritual practices, and in informal conversation.

[13] Consequently, political demands are not merely epistemological, but are also effected through an "ontological politics" (Mol 1998).

of the word, through new forms of agency and reinventions of the body) decolonial queer theory.[14] Therefore, decolonial queer theory is not an application of external categories formulated in the absence of stories like Cilene's, but instead movements of approximation and of opening toward theories and experiences that allow these forms of knowledge to affect and transform others. Any pretension of a decolonial queer theory implies an opening toward these other-theories, an opening which must take place in such a form and with such intensity as to be able to produce something new by the end of the voyage.

The End of the Voyage

Decolonial queer theory is therefore an encounter, a project, and a search. In developing this chapter, I have signaled a few simultaneous movements of the confluence and shock inherent in this encounter, and I have delineated key conceptual landscapes. I have described theoretical scenarios, while always travelling on voyages of theories and their intersections. In this process, a heterogeneous grouping of theories and authors has emerged in an area in which the very concepts of queerness and of decoloniality are still in dispute. Furthermore, these theories recall a variety of authors and traditions that do not always coincide.

Decolonial queer theory is a theoretical possibility that passes through our bodies, as well as through a politics of localization. Thinking as a *sudaca*, as a *bicha*,[15] thinking with a "theory of the asshole" and from the "asshole of the world" – to borrow Larissa Pelúcio's provocation – changes the texture of thought and the form of thinking; it alters questions, investigations, and problems (Pelúcio 2014a). To the extent to which decolonial queer theory can product something new, it does so by dislocating theories, delineating other logics, epistemologies, and ontologies, and causing them to emerge.

If this is truly the case, decolonial thinking must make queerness more attentive to the existence of a matrix of power that operates by naturalized racial and gender hierarchies; that allows for the reproduction of territorial and epistemological domination; and that obliterates experiences, forms of knowledge and forms of life. It is more vigilant than a structure that constructs and naturalizes a hierarchy of thought, and it treads cautiously in the intimate relationships between the epistemological and the colonial. Queer theory, for its part, shows how history has and continues to be written through hetero lenses; it shows that so much exists beyond the division of

---

[14] Within Trans* Studies – such as in Jay Prosser's work – there is a strong critique of theory queer utilizing trans* peoples' stories as examples of the instability of gender. I do not have space to discuss the theme here, but detailed critiques can be found in Prosser (1998). Cabral (2003) considers it indispensable to introduce the articulation of trans* theories and politics that both interpellate crystallized narratives and also introduce a demand for sexual citizenship in the first person.

[15] *Bicha*, like "queer," is used both pejoratively and as a term of self-affirmation for people of non-conforming gender and sexual identities. Its closest equivalent in American English would be somewhere between "queen" and "faggot."

masculine and feminine, beyond man and woman; it present other (re)inventions and possibilities of non-heteronormative sexualities; it shows that colonial logic is masculine, hetero, and white. But all of this occurs in simultaneous, related readings to the extent that queerness and decoloniality form a single theoretical movement, expanding our capacity for comprehension and perception.

Our challenge, then, is to read queer texts in a decolonial way, and – in the same way and with the same intensity – to queer texts that elucidate decolonial thinking. If the reading of bodies in the Global South is always radicalized and gendered, there is no way to act against the machine of coloniality by forgetting the multitude of queer bodies. In this part of the world, the condition of being queer is, equally, one of being decolonial. By stagnating ourselves in Theory without being affected by other-theories, queerness removes itself from its promised subversive character.

In different moments throughout this text, I have shown that, from a decolonial queer perspective, theory is not meant merely to be applied. Instead, our search is to fustigate the pedagogy that advocates for simple adhesion to the canon and affirms that the better we know and apply it, the more capable and (to use a term that is currently very fashionable) productive we will be. Decolonial queer theory disbelieves in this adhesion, and signals its assumptions and its geopolitical framing; it proposes a rereading of the Global North's theories in order to revise them, bend them, scrutinize their silences and obliterations, and to make them speak differently (as I have sought to show in my reading of Agamben). But searching also implies writing other-theories, allowing apparently strange and unfinished discourses, such as Cilene's, to affect the texture of thought. I think that the possibility of decolonial queer theory is linked to these investigations and to these worlds.

However, the key question here is not whether decolonial queer theory might pose questions to a shared, previously established theoretical framework (i.e., queerness and decoloniality), or elaborating the existence a variety of responses and forms of describing the world that ought to be collected, thereby augmenting their repertory and potential. Rather, the central question is how opening towards other-theories, such as Cilene's, presents the possibility of encounters with other questions and other worlds (and other bodies), to the extent that, as I have emphasized here, the political is not merely epistemological, but also ontological. In any case, neither queer theory nor decolonial thinking can serve as a mold for encapsulating these other-theories, these other histories.

Decolonial queer theory would therefore be composed of these movements, of itineraries in construction that are always open to other-theories. This opening highlights the centrality of the processes of translation, with the task of revising those epistemological categories that seek to universalize themselves through processes of unidirectional translation, thereby destabilizing preconceived notions. We can therefore come to understand translation as a process of transforming origin and destiny, and transforming concepts that travel.

This is how a queer decolonial theory emerges: it moves closer to these other-theories through its propositions of reading histories (other-histories) and other elaborations of agency, other reconstructions of bodies and sexualities, and other investigations of the naturalized hierarchies of knowledge. It indicates the silencings and obliterations of the theories of the Global North, making them speak differently and in another way. As I have said, this is a possibility, a search in this encounter of theories that travel. It is a provisional encounter, instable and disturbing, that makes these voyages of theories and concepts possible, in all their dissonances, problems, and potentials. It is provisional because, in the words of Saramago (1997), "the end of one voyage is only the beginning of another", since "the voyage never ends."

References

Agamben, G. (1998). *Quelche resta de Auschwitz: l'arquivio e il testimone*. Torino: Bollati Boringhieri.

Agamben, G. (2002). *Homo Sacer: o poder soberano e a vida nua*. Belo Horizonte: UFMG.

Agamben, G. (2004a). *Homo sacer: o poder soberano e a vida nua*. Belo Horizonte: UFMG.

Agamben, G. (2004b). *Estado de exceção*. São Paulo: Boitempo.

Agamben, G. (2005). *Lo abierto: el hombre y el animal*. Valéncia: Pretextos.

Agamben, G. (2006). Metropolis. *Generation online*. [Online]. Available at: http://www.generation-online.org/p/fpagamben4.htm. Acessed 20 June 2018.

Arendt, H. (1989). *Origens do totalitarismo*. São Paulo: Companhia das Letras.

Bento, B. (2014). Queer o quê? Ativismo e estudos transviados. *Cult, 193*, 43–46.

Bourdieu, P. (2002). Les conditions sociales de la circulation internationale des idées. *Actes de la recherche en sciences sociales, 145*, 3–8.

Butler, J. (1998). *Bodies that Matter: On the discursive limits of sex*. New York: Routledge.

Cabral, M. (2003). Ciudadanía (trans) sexual. Artículo sobre Tesis Premiada, Proyecto "Sexualidades salud y derechos humanos en América Latina". IESSDEH – Universidad Peruana Cayetano Heredia. [Online]. Available at: http://reconstruyendoelpensamiento.blogspot.com.ar/2008/04/ciudadana-trans-sexual-por-mauro-cabral.html. Acessed 17 June 2018.

Canfield, L. (2009). *Locating the Queer in Postcolonial/Decolonial Discourse: A Bibliographic Essay*. [Online]. Available at: http://ramsites.net/~ercanfield/assets/locatingthequeer_oggel_2009.pdf. Accessed: 22 June 2018.

Castro-Gomez, S. (2007). La Hybris del Punto Cero: Biopolíticas imperials y colonialidad del poder en la Nueva Granada (1750-1810). *Nómadas, 26*, 247–250.

Chakrabarty, D. (2000). *Provincializing Europe: postcolonial thought and the historical difference*. New Jersey: Princeton University Press.

Colling, L. (2015). *Que os outros sejam o normal: tensões entre movimento LGBT e ativismo queer*. Salvador: UFBA.

Connell, R. (2010). *Southern theory: The global dynamics of knowledge in social science*. Cambridge: Polity Press.

Córdoba, D. (2007). *Teoria Queer: políticas bolleras, maricas, trans, mestizas*. Barcelona: Egales.

Danielson, M. (2009). *Homecoming queers: Desire and difference in Chicana latina cultural production*. New Brunswick: N. J. Rutgers University Press.

Das, V. (2007). *Life and words: Violence and the descent into the ordinary*. Berkeley: University of California Press.

Driskill, Q.-L. (2010). Doubleweaving: Two-spirit critiques – building alliances between native and queer studies. *GLQ: A Journal of Lesbian and Gay Studies, 16*(1–2), 69–92.

Driskill, Q.-L., Finley, C., Gilley, B., & Morgensen, S. (2011). *Queer indigenous studies: Critical interventions in theory, politics, and literature*. Tucson: The University of Arizona Press.

Eaglestone, R. (2002). On Giorgio Agamben's Holocaust. *Paragraph: Journal of Modern Critical Theory, 25*, 52–67.

Esposito, R. (2010). On contemporary french and Italian political philosophy: An interview with Roberto Esposito. *Review*, (75), 109–117.

Ferguson, R. A. (2004). *Aberrations in black: toward a Queer of color critique*. Minneapolis: University of Minnesota.

Fernandes, E. R., & Arisi, B. (2017). *Gay indians in Brazil: Untold stories of the colonization of indigenous sexualities*. Cham: Springer International Publishing.

Fieldhouse, D. K. (1967). *The colonial empires: A comparative survey from the eighteenth century*. New York: Delacorte Press.

Grandmaison, O. L. C. (2005). *Coloniser, Exterminer: sur la guerre et l'état colonial*. Paris: Fayard.

Grosfoguel, R. (2006). From postcolonial studies to decolonial studies: Decolonizing postcolonial studies: A Preface. *Review, 29*, 141–142.

Guasch, O. (1998). *La sociedad rosa*. Barcelona: Anagrama.

Haraway, D. (2007). Le temoin modeste: diffractions feministes dans l'etude des sciences. In L. Allard, D. Gardey, & N. Magnan (Eds.), *Manifeste cyborg et autres essais. Sciences-Fictions-Féminismes* (pp. 209–333). Paris: Exils, Essais.

Hawley, J. C. (2001). *Post-colonial, Queer: Theoretical intersections*. Albany: Suny Press.

Hussain, N. (2003). *The jurisprudence of emergency: Colonialism and the rule of law*. Ann Arbor: University of Michigan Press.

Jiménez, R. M. (2002). *Sexualidades transgresoras. Una antología de estudios queer*. Barcelona: Icaria.

Johnson, E. P., & Henderson, M. G. (Eds.). (2005). *Black Queer studies: a Critical anthology*. Durham: Duke University Press.

Kalyvas, A. (2005). The sovereign weaver: beyond the camp. In A. Norris (Ed.), *Politics, metaphysics, and death: Essays on giorgio agamben's homo sacer* (pp. 107–134). Durham: Duke University Press.

Lentin, R. (2006). Femina sacra: Gendered memory and political violence. *Women's Studies International Forum, 29*, 463–473.

Lugarinho, M. C. (2001). *Como traduzir a teoria queer para a língua portuguesa* (Vol. 1, pp. 33–40). Gênero.

Lugones, M. (1987). Playfulness, 'World'-travelling, and loving perception. *Hypatia, 2*(2), 3–19.

Lugones, M. (2005). The coloniality of gender. *Worlds and knowledges otherwise*. [Online]. Available at: http://www.jhfc.duke.edu/wko/wko2.2genderanddecolonial.php. Acessed 20 June 2018.

Lugones, M. (2007). Heterosexualism and the Colonial/Modern gender system. *Hypatia, 21*, 186–209.

Lugones, M. (2011). Hacia un feminismo descolonial. *La manzana de la Discordia, 6*, 105–119.

Lugones, M. (2012). Subjetividad esclava, colonialidad de género, marginalidad y opresiones múltiples. In *Pensando los feminismos en Bolivia* (pp. 129–140). Conexión Fondo de Emancipación: La Paz.

Mahmood, S. (2001). Feminist theory, embodiment, and the docile agent: Some reflections on the Egyptian Islamic revival. *Cultural Anthropology, 16*, 202–236.

Maldonado-Torres, N. (2007). *Walter Mignolo: una vida dedicada al proyecto decolonial*. Bogotá: Universidad Central.

Mignolo, W. (1998). Postoccidentalismo: El argumento desde América Latina. In S. Castro-Gómez & E. Mendieta (Eds.), *Teorías sin disciplina: latinoamericanismo, poscolonialidad y globalización en debate* (pp. 26–46). Miguel Ángel Porrúa: México.

Mignolo, W. (2000). *Local Histories/Global designes. Coloniality, subaltern knowledges and border thinking*. New Jersey: Princeton University Press.

Mignolo, W. (2006). Citizenship, knowledge, and the limits of humanity. *American Literary History, 18*, 312–331.

Mignolo, W. (2007). *La idea de América Latina. La herida colonial y la opción decolononial*. Barcelona: Gedisa Editorial.

Mignolo, W. (2008). Desobediência epistêmica: a opção descolonial e o significado de identidade em política. *Cadernos de Letras da UFF, 34*, 287–324.

Miskolci, R. (2014a). Queering the geopolitcs of knowledge. In E. S. Lewis et al. (Eds.), *South-North dialogues on Queer epistemologies, embodiments and activisms* (pp. 13–30). Bern: Peter Lang.

Miskolci, R. (2014b). Um saber insurgente ao sul do Equador. *Periódicus, 1*, 43–67.

Miskolci, R., & Pelúcio, L. (2007). *Fora do Sujeito e Fora do Lugar: reflexões sobre performatividade a partir de uma etnografia entre travestis* (Vol. 7, pp. 257–267). Gênero.

Miskolci, R., & Pelúcio, L. (2017). Ao Sul da Teoria: notas sobre Teoria Queer e a geopolítica do conhecimento. In E. S. Lewis et al. (Eds.), *Queering Paradigms IV a: insurgências queer ao Sul do Equador* (pp. 69–90). Berna: Peter Lang.

Mol, A. (1998). Ontological politics: A word and some questions. In J. Law & J. Hassard (Eds.), *Actor network theory and after* (pp. 74–89). London: Blackwell.

Möser, C. (2013). *Féminismes en traductions: Théories voyageuses et traductions culturelles.* Paris: Editions des archives contemporaines.

Muñoz, J. E. (1999). *Disidentifications: Queers of color and the performance of politics.* Minneapolis: University of Minnesota Press.

Muñoz, J. E. (2006). Feeling brown, feeling down: Latina affect, the performativity of race, and the depressive position. *Signs: Journal of Women and Culture and Society, 31*(3), 675–688.

Ochoa, M. (2011). Diáspora Queer: mirada hemisférica y los estudios queer latino-americanos. In D. Balderston & A. Castro (Eds.), *Matute Cartografias queer: sexualidades y activismo LGBT en América Latina*. Pittsburgh: Instituto Internacional de Literatura Latinoamericana.

Ochoa, M. (2014). *Queen for a day. Transformistas, beauty Queens, and the performance of femininity in Venezuela.* Durham: Duke University Press.

Pelúcio, L. (2014a). Possible appropriations and necessary provocations for a Teoria Cu. In S. E. Lewis et al. (Eds.), *Queering paradigms IV South-North dialogues on Queer epistemologies, embodiments and activisms* (pp. 31–52). Oxford, EUA: Peter Lang Internacional Academic Publishers.

Pelúcio, L. (2014b). Traduções e torções ou o que se quer dizer quando dizemos queer no Brasil? *Revista Acadêmica Periódicus, 1*, 68–91.

Perez, E. (2003). Queering the Borderlands: The challenges of excavating the invisible and unheard. *Frontiers: A Journal of Women's Studies, 24*, 122–131.

Perez, E. (2014). Why do we need decolonial queer theories? *Conferência apresentada no encontro annual da American Studies Association*, Renaissance Hotel, Washington D.C., 28 Nov. 2014. Available at: http://citation.allacademic.com/meta/p314843_index.html. Accessed 20 June 2017.

Preciado, P. B. (2002). *Manifiesto contra-sexual: prácticas subversivas de identidad sexual.* Madrid: Pensamiento Opera Prima.

Prosser, J. (1998). *Second Skins. The body narratives of transsexuality.* New York: Columbia University Press.

Quijano, A. (1991). *Colonialidad y Modernidad/Racionalidad. Perú Indígena* (Vol. 29, pp. 11–21).

Quijano, A. (1998). La colonialidad del poder y la experiencia cultural latinoamericana. In R. Briceño-León & R. Heinz (Eds.), *Sonntag Pueblo, época y desarrollo: la sociología de América Latina* (pp. 139–155). Nueva Sociedad: Caracas.

Quijano, A. (2000). Colonialidad del poder, eurocentrismo y América Latina. In E. Lander (Ed.), *La Colonialidad del saber: Eurocentrismo y ciencias sociales. perspectivas latinoamericanas* (pp. 201–245). Caracas: Clasco.

Rivas, F. (2011). Diga 'queer' con la lengua afuera: sobre las confusiones del debate latino-americano. In Coordinadora Universitaria por la Disidencia Sexual (Ed.), *Por un feminismo sin mujeres: fragmentos de un segundo circuito disidencia sexual* (pp. 59–75). Santiago: Territores Sexuales Ediciones.

Sancho, F. (2014). *Desencuentros con lo queer/cuir. Cartón Piedra* (Vol. 127, pp. 20–23).

Saramago, J. (1997). *Viagem a Portugal.* São Paulo: Companhia das Letras.

Segato, R. L. (1998). The color-blind subject of Myth; or, Where to find Africa in the Nation. *Annual Review of Anthropology, 27*, 129–151.

Segato, R.L. (2006). Qué es un feminicídio. Notas para un debate emergente. *Mora, Revista del Instituto Interdisciplinar de Estudios de Gênero.* Brasília: Universidade Nacional de Brasília. Série Antropologia, 401. Available at: http://www.feminicidio.cl/jspui3/bitstream/123456789/344/1/segato.pdf. Acessed 20 June 2018.

Segato, R.L. (2012). Gênero e colonialidade: em busca de chaves de leitura e de um vocabulário estratégico descolonial. *E-cadernos ces*, 18, pp.106–131.

Segato, R.L. (2013). Ejes argumentales de la perspectiva de la Colonialidad del Poder. *Casa de las Américas*, 272, pp.1–5.

Segato, R. L. (2014). El sexo y la norma: frente estatal, patriarcado, desposesión, colonidad. *Estudos Feministas, 22*, 593–616.

Sharon, M. (2005). Queer theory for everyone: A review essay. *Signs: Journal of Women in Culture and Society, 31*, 191–218.

Shenhav, Y. (2012). Imperialism, exceptionalism and the contemporary world. In M. Svirsky & S. Bignall (Eds.), *Agamben and colonialism* (pp. 17–31). Edinburgh UP: Edinburgh.

Smith, A. (2010). Queer theory and native studies: The heteronormativity of settler colonialism. *GLQ: A Journal of Lesbian and Gay Studies, 16*(1–2), 42–68.

Soto, S. K. (2010). *Reading Chican@ like Queer: the De-mastery of Desire.* Austin: University of Texas.

Stoler, A. L. (1995). *Race and the education of desire: Foucault's history of sexuality and the colonial order of things.* Durham: Duke University Press.

Suriaga, E. V. (2011). Comentarios al dossier ¿Cómo se piensa lo 'queer' en América Latina? *Iconos. Revista de Ciencias Sociales, 40*, 119–127.

Walsh, C. (2004). Geopolíticas del conocimiento, interculturalidad y descolonialización. *Boletín ICCI-ARY Rimay, 6*, 1–2.

Walsh, C. (2009). *Interculturalidad, estado, sociedad: luchas (de)coloniales de nuestra época.* Quito: Universidad Andina Simón Bolívar.

Yarbro-Bejarano, Y. (1999). Sexuality and Chicana/o studies: Toward a theoretical paradigm for the twenty-first century. *Cultural Studies, 13*(2), 335–345.

Chapter 5
On the Poetics of Incorporation

Anyone who embarks on the torturous paths of themes of "the body" inevitably comes face-to-face with multiple definitions: the carnal situationality of modes of living; tensions below and beyond the skin; multi-connected, techno-living entities; the multiplicity of techniques of power and representation; and strange fictional politics. There is also the question of living flesh and of the place of subjectification, object, and subject; of organs managed by biopolitical regimes; of hierarchy and disposition in terms of race, difference of sex, and gender; of the locus of domination of corporal techniques and processes of internationalizing norms; and of the potency that makes the incorporation of genders possible, a potency that acts, performs, and is performed. Latour (2004, p. 227) affirmed that "there is a *life* for the body after science studies and feminism, but it is not the same life as before", calling attention to the centrality that this theme has been accorded in the social sciences. This centrality, according to Latour, is due to encounters between feminism, studies of science, reinterpretations of Foucault, and the expansion of bioindustry.

Throughout this chapter – which, to a certain extent, is mobilized by these definitions[1] – I will also return to the body in order to formulate the following questions: What articulations construct bodies? If bodies are interfaces that become descriptive once they have learned to be affected by multiple elements, put into movement by human and non-human entities, what are these affects, these entities, and these mediators? How do these incorporations occur? How does a body invent itself? Reflecting on these inquiries based both on my own research and on pedagogical experiences – along with the use of filmic images and narratives – I will aim to entangle myself within the processes of invention of the bodies of *travestis*.

These questions began to arise for me between 1998 and 2000, when I carried out ethnographic research in an institution for AIDS patients. It was there that I first came into contact with *travestis'* own constructions within Afro-Brazilian religions

---

[1] Here, I refer to authors such as Butler (1990, 1993, 2004), Haraway (1991), Mauss (1973), Mol (1999, 2002) and Preciado (2002, 2008, 2009).

P. P. G. Pereira, *Queer in the Tropics*, SpringerBriefs in Sociology,
https://doi.org/10.1007/978-3-030-15074-7_5

(Pereira 2004; 2012). Later, I coordinated a research project on therapeutic itineraries among *travestis* in Santa Maria, a city in the state of Rio Grande do Sul, in southern Brazil. It was through this context – as an ethnographic agent within a fieldwork that "does not have a right moment to begin [or to] end" (Peirano 2014, p.379) – and as part of my effort to reflect on how inquiries from that time period had affected me that this chapter arose. Here, I must emphasize three especially important references that showed me the necessity of examining certain events that I had experienced: first, an interview for pedagogical purposes that I carried out at the Center for References and Defense of Diversity (CRDD); second, a documentary about *bombação*[2] that a public health doctor gave me; and finally, photographs exchanged among *mothers-* and *fathers-of-saints* from Candomblé religious practices during another of my research projects. These movements not only allowed me to grow closer to *travestis'* own experiences, but also to understand something of their stylistic economy, fabrication of beauty, and the invention of complex forms of incorporation in their experiences of transit and flux.

Body and Biomedicine

Located on Rua Major Sertório, in São Paulo, Brazil, CRDD is a space intended to serve men and women, sex workers, gay people, *travestis* and other trans* people, and people living with HIV/AIDS in conditions of "social risk" or "vulnerability". Amidst a hardened landscape of old and often degraded buildings, the institution takes in people whose "difference" makes it difficult or impossible for them to be attended to within the general confines of the Brazilian Public Health System.

   In 2011, with the intention of learning more about CRDD's history, I arranged to interview Irina Karla Bacci, who was then coordinator of the institution. My idea was to produce a filmed interview to be shown to medical students at the Federal University of São Paulo (Unifesp) so as to reinforce a classroom discussion about difference and health. During the interview, which lasted for approximately 30 min, Bacci spoke about CRDD's history, starting from its beginnings in the context of the fight against AIDS. She also said that "prejudice and discrimination" form a significant barrier that makes it difficult for trans* people, gays, and lesbians to access Brazil's public health services. She added that even when trans*, gay, and lesbian people manage to access the health system, they are almost always discriminated against and subject to all sorts of violence. According to Bacci, "regardless of social class, of access to schools and familial support – or lack thereof – when [gay, lesbian, and trans* populations] need health services, they generally have problems". CRDD's task, therefore, is to address these problems.

---

[2] Very roughly, the slang term *bombação* translates somewhere between "pumping" and "bombing;" it refers to amateur aesthetic surgery carried out with industrial-grade silicone, further elucidated on pages 4–5. *Bombação* will not be translated in the text, nor will *bombadeira,* the term used to refer to someone who administers such surgery.

Bacci described how doctors react to the demands and mobilizations of LGBTQIA+ people, and how these processes altered their protocols and their resolve. For example, doctors often become more attentive to trans* men, or more receptive to assisted reproduction among single women or homosexual couples. Based on everyday cases, the coordination of CRDD keeps detailed records of the actions of public health services in administering hormones, mastectomies, and prostheses. For Bacci, medicine and health services serve as a locus of oppression, control, and prejudice at the same time as they offer spaces for the demands, struggles, and conquests of LGBTQIA+ people.

At a certain point in the interview, Bacci's narrative addressed the construction of *travestis'* bodies. At first, she suggested that *travestis'* bodies are also reappropriations of and detours to medical discourses. She did not say so explicitly, but her arguments appeared to take for granted a very familiar decision among CRDD members: namely, taking feminine hormones (estrogen) and birth control (estrogen and progesterone). In most cases, these hormones are administered by more experienced *travestis* who not only advise how to take them and where to buy them, but who also advise about side effects. It is a slow apprenticeship in techniques of taking hormones and in manipulating medical instruments (such as syringes and needles). New users do not know the adequate dosage of these substances, or how to combine them; their questions most often center around which hormones ought to be administered[3] (and how) so as to conform to a feminine body.

Bacci also commented on *travestis'* use of industrial silicone as a means of changing their bodies and adding contours. This substance, originally developed for industrial and electrical uses, has never been recommended for soft tissue implants. Liquid silicone became popular after World War II, and *travestis* consider it to be a fast and low-cost method for changing their bodies' contours. The ease of access, coupled with the extreme poverty in which *travestis* often live, justifies the intense use of a practice that biomedicine recommends avoiding entirely, given that it may result in serious complications that are difficult to treat.

To describe a body produced and reproduced by techniques and substances, Bacci narrated stories of processes of incorporation[4] that utilize dislocating

---

[3] *Travestis* without access to endocrinologists often use contraceptives that they obtain from pharmacies. They frequently take elevated doses of synthetic estrogen and progesterone (with anti-ovulation functions), especially ethinyl estradiol and cyproterone acetate pills or else monthly estradiol enanthate and algestone acetophenide injections. The hormonal regimen that associates drugs with anti-adrogenic effects – which, according to bio-medical formulations, is responsible for inhibiting "masculinizing" action, the hormone responsible for maintaining the secondary sexual characteristics of men – to hormones considered to be "feminizing", such as the progesterone in pills that contain cyproterone acetate (Galindo, Pimentel and Vilela 2013). However, healthcare professionals advise that the doses of estrogen and progesterone contained in these anti-ovulation hormonal regimens can lead to blocking the secretion of endogenous (testicular) testosterone, and, as a result, a diminished libido. Regarding hormones, see: García-Becerra (2009), Oudshoorn (1994) and Sanabria (2013).

[4] I intend to argue that the term "incorporation" and its derivatives (such as "incorporate" and "corporification") cannot account for a variety of meanings attached to the conformation of the body (or, at best, can only partially account for these meanings), at least insofar as they relate to the experience upon which I aim to reflect here.

technologies so as to produce something more. For example, *travestis* utilize hormones intended to control feminine fertility in order to change their bodies according to their own desires, in a movement that appropriates and reconfigures normalizing technologies. Thus, industrial silicone, intended for use as a lubricant, materializes in buttocks and thighs (Benedetti 2005; Duque 2011; Pelúcio 2005; 2006; Preciado 2008).

Because these processes of corporal change are not beyond adversity, Bacci spoke next about "health problems." After mentioning that hormones provoke fatigue, sleepiness, and a reduction of sexual desire, she claimed that "among *travestis*, the industrial silicone in their thighs, usually put there by *bombadeiras*, falls [down their bodies]." Furthermore, she said, "it is not uncommon for *travestis* to arrive at CRDD with silicone in their feet."

Bombadeiras are people who apply industrial silicone for physical uses; often, they are more experienced *travestis*. Because of the technical difficulties of the procedures, these *bombadeiras* must be specialists, knowledgeable in the "schemes of the trade," as I heard on one occasion. Industrial silicone application can often be described as follows[5]: as a *bombadeira* conducts the process, the *travesti* undergoing the *bombação* lies in bed and receives dozens of industrial silicone injections in the parts of her body that she wishes to modify (The most common areas are thighs, breasts, and buttocks). The procedure rarely takes place under anesthetic. During these sessions, the *travesti* remains supine for 8–12 h, depending on the quantity of silicone to be injected and the body part she has chosen to modify. Her body is tied with strips of nylon stockings, which are rolled together and held close to injection sites so as to prevent the liquid from running; this procedure forms scars, calling attention to the fabric tied around the body. Soon after the industrial silicone is inserted, the orifices are closed with instant glue (Souza 2013).

As I have already mentioned, there are recurring recounts of silicone "slippage," especially in the legs and feet. The process can also lead to circulatory problems such as varicose veins, hypertension, and diabetes. Complications after injections of liquid industrial silicone range from alterations in skin color and consistency (such as the formation of nodes and granulomas) to inflammatory processes (such as necrosis, ulcerations, abscesses, fistulas, retractions, and scarring deformations). In the absence of health services, these problems do not receive sufficient therapeutic attention, given that health care professionals do not usually relate them to the use of silicone. According to Bacci, this frequently leads to two situations: either doctors who do not think of removing the silicone; or who, once they perceive the silicone to be causing problems, send *travestis* to hospitals or other health care centers where they are met with violence. Frequently, these situations lead to thrombosis, amputations, and other complications. This is one of the numerous examples of the distance that exists between health care services and the needs of *travesties*.[6]

---

[5] I describe the following scene based both on the interview with Bacci and on my own research experiences.

[6] In her investigation, Duque (2011, p. 98) notes that the forms that *travestis* use to alter their bodies are changing, and that plastic surgery is gradually substituting silicone and needles. She argues that *bombadeiras* may cease to exist in the near future. However, Bacci's discussions at CRDD, as well as my own research experiences, suggest that industrial silicone is still in widespread usage.

Based on *travestis*' extreme difficulties in gaining access to even minimally attentive health care, the role of CRDD is to mediate, to search for solutions, to establish dialogue with health care services, to call attention to differences, and to find partners that are at least somewhat sensitive to including bodies and souls that have been jettisoned from the official medical system. By understanding the specificity of the continuous construction of dissident bodies, CRDD sustains the possibility of inserting these bodies into spaces that understand the body as a given. This exercise necessarily presupposes a continuous learning process. There are always creative forms of accessing health care services, of obtaining desired corporal changes, and of understanding hormone administration, among other thing. "In order to be a *travesti*", according to one *travesti* with whom I spoke at the entrance to CRDD, "you have to have tricks".[7] The term signals to an ample semantic field composed of expressions like artifice, strategy, and subterfuge. It also appears to be adequate for the strategies involved in inventing bodies, and in confronting biomedicine as it operates in accordance with fictions that regulate bodies. These "tricks" do not seek to repudiate medicine (which *travestis* often consider to be external and homogenous), but rather to scour for openings and lapses, to construct spaces, to find the agency possible for emerging forms of life within these biomedical regimes (Stryker 2015).

Bacci's narrative is striking because of the confluence of *bombadeiras* intervening in and with bodies, together with public policies that prove to be more or less effective. It is striking because of her references to hormones and medical procedures, to disputes for health services, and to violence. It is especially striking when she spoke the following, in the deep voice of a *"daughter-of-a-saint"*: I am *Iaô*, daughter of *Xangô*, made and shorn[8]; *Odú Kètà*, with 5 years of obligation paid. Bacci frequents the *terreiro*[9] of Pai Marcelo D'Oxossi, and her godfather is Pai Fernando Quaresma de Xangô.

The Designed Body

For 3 years, I showed my interview with Bacci to medical students in my classes at Unifesp. In addition to the interview, our classroom discussions focused on a research project that I carried out with Martha Souza regarding *travestis*' itineraries in the Public Health System in Santa Maria, in Rio Grande do Sul (Souza 2013; Souza and Pereira 2015; Souza et al. 2015). Both sources presented similar issues: violence, stigmatization, and the various failures of health care systems in attending

---

[7] The Portuguese word "artimanhas" most closely translates to "tricks", but it does not carry the same insinuation of sex work as the English term.

[8] Formal initiation in Candomblé sects usually involves head shaving.

[9] The term *terreiro* designates the religious space of Afro-Brazilian religions. It is a space with its own distinct rituals, relationships, and social dynamics. I hope that, as the text progresses, this first brief mention of these religions will not appear to have come at random.

to *travestis*, either through impeding their care outright, or else by producing inadequate forms of receiving *travestis* as patients.

Both the interview that I conducted and the research projects I coordinated engaged medical students as well as faculty and staff members, and this engagement became noticeable throughout Unifesp. Perhaps as a result, Professor Luiz Cecílio, a public health doctor, gave me *Bombadeira*, a 2007 documentary directed by Luiz Carlos de Alencar. Luiz Cecílio was certainly attuned to the importance that my classroom discussions held for the medical school, in examining multiple important themes: difference and health; processes of health and sickness; social determinates of health; and "specific forms of attention to the trans* population within the health-care system". And, of course, he was right.

Bombadeira tells the stories of *bombação* among *travestis* in the city of Salvador, in Bahia state, northeastern Brazil. Watching it, I immediately thought of my conversation with Bacci, as well as of the physical changes among *travestis* that I witnessed while conducting research in Santa Maria. I also recalled previous discussions regarding differentiated forms of attending to patients in Public Health Systems. In certain scenes of the documentary, *travestis* articulate a harsh critique of the care they receive from the Public Health Systems, amplifying what Bacci explained during my interview with her. One especially noteworthy example from the film is Leila's indignation at the attention that *travestis* receive in hospitals: "Public hospitals don't do silicone implants, as much as we want them to. They don't even want to take them out; imagine putting them in!". In response to the same issue, Michelle explains:

> They won't easily take [industrial silicone] out. You need to be near death for them to remove it, so can you imagine them putting it in? Because [putting prostheses in] is an aesthetic surgery [according to Public Health Services]. So, they charge money for a service like that, understand?! They won't do it, unless it's going to kill us! Because it's dangerous for them to do it. To kill [those girls], to see them writhing around like a chicken with its head cut off. I believe that some of them do that.

These indignations were the same as many that, inspired by my interview with Bacci, I raised in the classroom with medical students over the course of several years. Should public health services put in prosthetics for and consider administering hormones to *travestis*? These questions always inspired polemical arguments. Leila and Michelle's harsh critiques raised a question of extreme importance in the field of Brazilian public health: they denounced the perceived subjectivity in the bodies of *travestis*, who are often left to die (Carrara and Vianna 2006; Peres 2005). *Travestis* are seen as having precarious lives that are unworthy of maintaining; after all, where there is no life, there cannot be death[10] (Butler 2005, 2009). There is a

---

[10] These formulations show how interventions that aim to modify gender and sex are constituted within a privileged perspective in order to reflect on the problems and inadequacies of the Unified Health System [Sistema Único de Saúde (SUS)], as shown by García-Becerra (2009); additionally, they show the possibilities of constructing appropriate forms of attention and care. In *Bombadeira*, Leila and Michelle make direct appeals to (and direct demands of) the founding principles of Brazil's Public Health System, which include the universality, equality, and completeness of healthcare.

relationship between subjectivity and *bombação*: namely, an artifice created between precariousness and desire, as seen in the documentary *Bombadeira*. In one scene from the film, Celine explains the central role of the *bombadeira*:

> *Travestis* can only change their bodies with the help of this *bombadeira*. She becomes the only way out, the only escape, the only hope for this *travesti*, for this transsexual. Because prosthetics and physical change – getting prosthetics through conventional means – is very expensive. So the role of the *bombadeira* is very important…for *travestis*, not for society.

In following *travestis*' own stories, *Bombadeira* highlights the acts of *bombação*. In this scene, the film's subjects relate their own opinion of *bombação*. Describing their relationship to the risks of this intense physical intervention, as well as explaining their own motivations in seeking it. They also describe the transformations that take place after such procedures. When the film shows *bombação* in action, the camera is held at such an angle as to delicately exclude the images of the faces of both the *travesti* receiving industrial silicone injection and the *bombadeira* applying them (Braga 2015).

The filmic narrative allows the *travestis*' to express their own formulations without reducing them to exoticized caricatures of themselves. Besides – or perhaps because of– this vision, the documentary deconstructs an image of *bombação* and of other changes in *travestis*' bodies as mistaken or exclusively negative. The camera refuses to approach *travestis* exclusively as vulnerable subjects or as health problems unto themselves; instead, it illustrates their personal stories, their dramas, and their fears. It relates physical transformation to desire and to "beauty pain" as part of the construction of bodies, as desire that becomes flesh. Samara, one of the film's subjects, explains:

> Beauty pain is a ripping pain. And there the girl is, in pain, taking it. But she knows it'll make her pretty. It's beauty pain – that's what we call it, right, sister? It's beauty pain, like dyeing your hair, or pulling something into you, or piercing your ear; that's all beauty pain. So that's what they say: "It's beauty pain, sister". If you feel the pain, if it's burning, you have to feel the burning, but you have to take it. They give you anesthetic, but even with anesthetic, you feel it going into you. They say you feel it burning into you.

Pain, together with desire, acts on the body. It is related to the possibility of reinventing the body; it is "the body drawn in oil," as I heard at a certain time. Perhaps because it perceives this potency, and makes evident the poetics of corporal construction, the film produces important analyses that highlight modes of resistance and "the courageous invention of existences". The documentary's language approaches the body as a place of experiences, to the extent that images of *bombação* strive to discover potency capable of surpassing fear and pain (Braga 2015; Alvarenga Pereira 2015).

Yet there is something in the *travestis*' stories throughout the documentary that does not fit neatly into theories that ascribe their corporal transformations to subversion. Their narratives certainly demonstrate that the body is not passive, not a given upon which biopower acts; instead, it is a potency that makes possible the incorporation of genders. In their relations to medicine, the actions of *travestis*' signaled their capacity to intervene in biotechnological *dispositifs* of corporal production and sexual subjectivity (Pereira 2008a, b; 2012; Preciado 2002, 2009). But if the body is engendered within these relationships and negotiations (with health services, drugs, and industrial artifacts), there is also a dimension that points toward other types of assemblage that the *travestis* in *Bombadeira* insist on emphasizing: namely, their relationship to Afro-Brazilian religions.[11]

At the very beginning of the documentary, Andrezza tells how she arrived in São Paulo; immediately afterward, she mentions that she became sick, which led her to spend 9 days in an intensive care unit. There, she was diagnosed with meningitis and pneumonia, a diagnosis with which Andrezza never disagreed, and for which she followed the prescribed course of medical treatment. However, she also sought out other explanations (and formulated her own) as to what had happened. The story of these explanations is fascinating.

The first fortuneteller that Andrezza consulted assured her that her sickness was a result of spiritual "work": someone was trying to kill her. This kind of "work" is serious in Brazil: it involves sorcery, prayers, and cures. For Afro-Brazilian religions, it is a magical-religious rite, a ritual that intervenes in events, resolving problems, afflictions, and illnesses (Maggie 1992; Montero 1986a, b;), or else provoking disorder and interfering directly in worldly events. (Prandi 1991) Andrezza, who was aware of this capacity for intercession, was afflicted; the story made her want to learn more about what had happened to her, so she sought out a woman who could tell her. In Andrezza's words: "Then her Iansã took over. She told me everything, and I didn't say a word. She said: 'Go to so-and-so's house and she'll tell you what's going on.'" Following these instructions, Andrezza went to Dona Nininha, who revealed to her a complex web of "works," predictions, and prophesies.

> So I go to so-and-so's house. Dona Nininha, something like that, over there in Pero Vaz. Then this woman told me everything. She said that it was my grandmother, my grandmother's neighbor (who was still alive). My mom's mother, when she was still alive…when my mom was dating my father, my grandmother always fought with this neighbor. They didn't get along. They fought. So while they were fighting, the daughters (meaning my mom and my aunts) always wound up being part of the story. So in one of these fights, Mom and Dad were still dating. So in one of these fights, Dona Rodelice [the neighbor] said: "Just you wait: when you have a son, he's going to be a faggot."

According to Andrezza's narrative, her family frequently had misunderstandings with Rodelice, their neighbor. In one of these arguments, her grandmother said: "See? You said he was going to be [a faggot], but he isn't". The neighbor responded: "I'm going to show you that, when he returns, […] he's travelling now, […], he's going to become a woman". Andrezza's grandmother searched for someone who could undo this "work", but this person reaffirmed that Andrezza would, in fact,

---

[11] I will emphasize here that the documentary's principal objective is not to explore relationships between religion and the body. Nevertheless, these relationships appear inadvertently and become as central to the film as the process of *bombação* itself. According to Goldman (2015), Afro-Brazilian religions form a conjuncture that is heteroclitic but consistently articulate; they include religious practices and conceptions based on forms brought by enslaved African people, and also incorporate elements of indigenous cosmology and practices, folk Catholicism, and European spiritism.

become a woman. Her grandmother returned to talk to the neighbor, not in order to undo the "work", but instead to kill Andrezza during her travels. The objective was to "make work" in order for Andrezza to "die over there" so as "not [to] ... bring shame on the family". Because the neighbor refused, Andrezza's grandmother sought out someone else whose "work" would make Andrezza die. Based on this story of predictions and violence, Andrezza assures us that she didn't die in São Paulo because the *orixás*[12] would not allow it.

The efforts of her grandmother and her grandmother's neighbor did not work, and Andrezza did not die. When she arrived in São Paulo, as she herself puts it: "Oh, my love! It was strong [work], you know? I transformed into a marvelous woman". She explains that the *orixás* give her lots of strength, support, and security, and that every *travesti* has a *pomba-gira*. In Andrezza's case, the *orixás* not only allowed her to live, helping her to leave the hospital in spite of her serious illnesses; they also produced her woman's body. She transformed into a "marvelous woman", thanks to hormones, silicone, to the corporal techniques she learned, the various aesthetic procedures she underwent, and, above all, because of the enchantments and strength of the *orixás*.

However, the actions of *orixás* and other entities are not predictable. Over the course of the documentary, another very strong subject, Leila, tells of her own experience, which is very different from Andrezza's. In spite of her relationship to the *orixás*, Leila avoids going to Candomblé. As she explains:

> I have my *orixás*, understand? I try really hard not to go to Candomblé. I refuse my calling, but I don't go, because I have my "slaves". I have lots of saints. I have a male "slave," and he's very, very ... when he took me over here, he left me naked, naked here in my house. And if I don't close this door, folks say he's going to come out. So I try really hard not to go to Candomblé because of him, because sometimes we have a *orixá*, a man, a male slave who won't let us put silicone in our chests. Because when I put [silicone] in, I had to withdraw, understand? I had to isolate myself from Candomblé.

These spiritual entities act in conflict with Leila's wishes. A male "slave" can prevent a *travesti* from constructing her body as she desires. There are even stories of a *travesti* who "pumped up her chest" and was punished, as related by Mara Chicotada (also known as Pai Neném):

> A *travesti* who was of *axé*[13] died when she pumped up her breasts. She was persecuted because of what happened. A *caboclo* came, took a knife, and shoved it into her heart. And it went all the way through her heart and came out the other side. Because she pumped up her chest, and he wouldn't accept it. And that's what I'm afraid of: that one [entity] will accept it but that another won't accept it, won't want it.

Therefore, even in case of a negative – in other words, when a *travesti* does not change her body – it is *exus* (including *caboclos*, *pretos-velhos*, *pomba-giras*) and

---

[12] *Orixás* are divinities associated with Afro-Brazilian religions. In the context of Afro-Brazilian religions, the words "saint" and "*orixá*" are generally synonymous. (T.N.)

[13] *Axé* (asé) is both a spiritual life force in Yoruba cosmology and a common blessing word, roughly equivalent to "amen". Being "of *axé*" implies belonging to an Afro-Brazilian religions practice. (T.N.)

orixás who define what one can do, how one can do it, and when. Even *bombadeiras* have to obey *orixás*. For some of the *travestis* with whom I spoke, knowing how to listen to *orixás* and *exus* is part of *bombação*; listening to them forms an action integrated with the rest of the process. Leila recalls a *travesti* who asked her for a silicone injection, but advised that her *orixá* was opposed to the procedure. Given that she herself could not undergo silicone implants for the same reasons, Leila refused to perform them on this other *travesti*:

> She herself told me that her *orixá* didn't want her to, but that she wanted it. So I said: "I'm really sorry, but I'm not going to do it. I know that I have this same problem". I told her: "For you to do it, you have to remove yourself [from religious practice]". She said: "But I can't do that, because it's how I make money". So I told her that, in this case, I wouldn't put silicone [in her]. I know that she managed to put [the silicone] in, but I didn't do it! It was another *bombadeira*.

As we can see, there are many different forms of agency involved in constructing *travestis'* bodies. The body is brought into being through performances, through the imaginative reinvention of biomedical technologies (such as hormones and prostheses), as well as through the slow learning process of intervention techniques (such as the needles and nylon ties involved in *bombação*). This is why *travestis* speak of subversion (schemes, artifices, and strategies). The body also comes about through contact with unpredictable substances that produce pain, malaise, and side effects that are disagreeable and bothersome, and that are applied in actions that reach the limits of this unpredictability.

However, as we can gather from these stories, the construction of *travestis'* bodies does not depend only on hormones, silicone, or biomedical and corporal techniques; it is also based on the relationships between people and spiritual entities. These relationships take place among families, among neighbors, and in religious settings. They take place both among *travestis* and between *travestis* and *caboclos*, *pomba-giras*, *bombadeiras*, hormones, and silicone, all acting together in inventing bodies. In Andrezza's case, for example, the production of her body began to take shape before she was born, through familial relations, and because of a conflict among neighbors. In her narrative, the *orixás* allow her to live, in spite of the "work" and of predictions made to the contrary. And it is these same entities who produced her as a "beautiful woman".

At the exact moment that I write this sentence, I recall the *travestis* in Santa Maria who, in a different context than those shown in *Bombadeira,* seek spaces in which they can dance in "saints' houses" and incorporate *pomba-giras*. After all, as Andrezza put it: "every *travesti*, every gay man, has a *pomba-gira*, a [Maria] Padilha [One of the many names of *pomba-giras*]".

Delivering the Body

Although my work on the insertion of *travestis* in Afro-Brazilian religions began with my ethnography at CRDD between 1998 and 2000, the intensity of the connection between *travestis* and *pomba-giras* truly struck me 12 years later, during my aforementioned research in Santa Maria. In our attempts to follow the paths of *travestis* through the Brazilian public health care system, Martha Souza and I quickly perceived both their problems in being attended to by public institutions as well as the significant daily difficulties that they confronted in dealing with official public health services. Following their searches for basic care led us to *terreiros*; to Quimbanda sessions; to mothers- and fathers-of-saints who were themselves *travestis*; and to other spaces that took in *travesties*.[14] I recognize that *pomba-giras* are treated with reverence in Candomblé and Umbanda throughout Brazil, especially by impoverished urban populations who seek them out to help resolve afflictions linked to desire and sexuality (Prandi 1996, p. 140). However, the *travestis* in Santa Maria seem to have an even more intimate relationship with these entities.

In 2013, already in the midst of our research, Martha Souza sent me a series of images of *travestis* participating in Quimbanda sessions, photographed by fathers- and mothers-of-saints, as well as by Martha herself. I soon recognized that the majority of participants were *travestis* who were "mounted[15]" or who were embodying *pomba-giras*. I was especially struck by one particular photograph, not only because of its visual beauty, but also by the features of the people pictured. The photograph shows the bent-over form of someone's seminude back, delineating movement. The person pictured is wearing black and yellow, colors associated with Maria Padilha: the most popular *pomba-gira*, the spirit of a very beautiful and seductive woman (Augras 2001; Capone 2004; Meyer 1993). A tiara hold back the subject's black hair, and a pendant – neither small nor large – hangs about the figure's neck, showing off the body's movements, while downward-glancing eyes show an absorbed countenance. A thin man appears before Maria Padilha – also wearing black and yellow, along with a very well placed white hat – singing and dancing. This is Zé Pelintra, a *malandro*[16] known to be transgressive, astute, and involved in prohibited practices (Augras 2009). The photo was taken during a Quimbanda session in the Rio Grande do Sul, in Bagé, a city approximately 150 miles (250 kilometers) away from Santa Maria. Xuca (Pai Ricardo de Iemanjá) and Maicon were the figures photographed incorporating Maria Padilha and Zé Pelintra. Xuca is a *travesti* who, in 2013, was approximately 30 years old; Iemanjá

---

[14] There is a relatively substantial existing literature regarding dissident bodies and Afro-Brazilian religions, beginning with Fry (1977; 1982) and followed by other important names (Birman 1985; 1995; 2005; Leão Teixeira 2000; Santos 2008; Segato 1995). However, Santos (2013) show how some priests and priestesses have reproduced heteronormative positions in relation to the femininity of *travestis* and trans* women.

[15] *Montada* ("mounted") carries implications both of being "dolled up", but also of being possessed or undergoing a process of spiritual incorporation.

[16] *Malandros* or *pelintras* were originally Umbanda entities; currently, they are also found in other Afro-Brazilian religions, such as Candomblé.

is her *"head saint"* and Oxalá is her *"body saint"*.[17] She was married to Maicon de Oxalá Obokun, a *babalorixá*.[18]

A *pomba-gira* is a feminine *exu*, the spirit of a woman who was a prostitute in life; a woman capable of dominating men with her schemes. In the ritual language of Angola Candomblés (of the Bantu tradition), the name of this *exu* is Bongbogirá; pombagira (*pomba-gira*) is a derivation of the original word[19] (Augras 1989). The term *pomba-gira* is suggestive of the entity's ambiguity: *gira*, a word of Bantu origin, suggests both the Portuguese verb *girar* (to turn) and the ritual circle; *pomba*, in addition to designating a pigeon in Portuguese, also refers to genital organs (masculine in northeastern Brazil and feminine in the south). Therefore, the name is charged both with ambiguousness as well as with sexual references (Augras 1989).

Pomba-giras[20] are corporifications of transgressive femininity; they have the power to avenge and to offer care (Hayes 2011). They are most closely related to "women and homosexuals", because people who "receive" a *pomba-gira* through a state of trance – whether they are women or men – transform, for a time, into ultrafeminine queens, seductresses, and foul-mouthed prostitutes (Hayes 2011).[21]

Xuca and Maicon frequent the saint's house of Pai Fernando de Xangô, another father-of-a-saint, whose saint's house has a relatively long history and is one of the best structured in Santa Maria. Pai Fernando maintains that the close link between *travestis* and *pomba-giras* stems from the entities' own forms of action: *pomba-giras* "bring movement and happiness" and act "in the changes in the *travestis'* bodies. She [the *pomba-gira*] is part of the woman who arises". *Travestis* frequent Pai Fernando's house, especially during Quimbanda sessions, perhaps because the mediums in these sessions – possessed by the *pomba-giras* that come into physical being through the bodies of women, gay men, and *travestis* – take on provocative sexual behaviors (Capone 2004). The *travestis* arrive at the house after midnight,

---

[17] I heard the following explanation regarding "head saints" and "body saints" (or *orixá* of the head and *orixá* of the body): the "head saint" is the principal entity, responsible for the personal, physical, and moral characteristics of the son- or daughter-of-a-saint, whereas the "body saint" is the *orixá* of the body's partner, also known as "adjunct".

[18] When I saw this image, I immediately hoped to use it as the cover for a book that, in 2014, I was in the process of publishing (Pereira 2014). I asked Xuca and Maicon, who agreed at once. As soon as the book was printed, I sent them a copy; they thanked me for "respecting the entities", an important factor considering their "many years of living with each other, an entire history together". Xuca, holding forth on the central place that Maria Padilha occupies in her life, added that "the *pomba-gira* opens paths".

[19] In Portuguese, "pomba-gira" literally means "pigeon-turn".

[20] *Pomba-giras* are multiple and unique. Each has her own specific name, appearance, preferences, symbols, and songs. Among the most well-known *pomba-giras* are: Pombagira *Rainha* (Queen); Maria Padilha; Pombagira *Sete Saias* (Seven Skirts); Maria Molambo; Pombagira *da Calunga*; Pombagira Cigana ("Gypsy"); Pombagira *do Cruzeiro* (of the Cross); Pombagira *Cigana dos Sete Cruizeiros* ("Gypsy" of the Seven Crosses); Pombagira *das Almas* (Pombagira of the Souls); Pombagira Maria Quitéria; Pombagira *Dama da Noite* (Lady of the Night); Pombagira *Menina* (Girl); Pombagira *Mirongueira* (Enchantress) (Prandi 1996).

[21] For further analyses of the *pomba-gira*, see: Augras (1989); Birman (2005); Contins (1983); Contins and Goldman (1984); Guimarães (2001); Hayes (2011); Meyer (1993) and Prandi (1996).

"mounted" with their *pomba-giras*, as in the aforementioned photo of Xuca and Maicon.

That beautiful image – a snapshot of the relationship between Maria Padilha and Xuca, as well as between Zé Pelintra and Maicon – shows the interwoven ties that exist between entities and fathers-of-saints. Over time, one can see that these interwoven ties stem from specific personal relationships that have been painstakingly constructed between entities and mediums, between *travestis* and *pomba-giras*. Through these relationships, entities and mediums construct links and live out conflicts. In other words, there is a continuous and mutual elaboration between future and past in mediums' experiences with spiritual entities (Rabelo 2008, p. 113). To say that the *pomba-gira* "opens paths", as Xuca did is to sustain a history of relationships, to presuppose the existence of a shared future, to wager on the links and constructions between entities and *travestis* that are made and remade on a variety of paths and itineraries.

One of the most assiduously faithful *travestis* in Pai Fernando's house is Morgana, a 46-year-old mother-of-a-saint born and raised in Santa Maria. She lives with her "saint's family," sharing her home only with people who are "of the religion" (in this case, her husband and her children-of-a-saint). Morgana became a mother-of-a-saint in 2014, but she says that she has been "of the religion for almost my whole life". Having been raised by her father-of-a-saint, the only family she knew was her "saint's family". Like Andrezza in *Bombadeira*, Morgana speaks of an important event in her life: a grave illness that could have "knocked her down" had it not been for the fact that her "faith was great", her *pomba-gira* was strong, and she "would not fall". In fact, she is totally recuperated. Morgana attributes her health and her joie de vivre to her *pomba-gira*: "The *pomba-gira* ... is the lady who orders things to be done, who makes things happen at the crossing, in the crossroads. She's the lady who brings us good life, who brings us well-being". Morgana has incorporated the *pomba-gira* for years, and she says: "I give my body, my soul, and my heart to her, because I know that ... she will bring good things to me and to whoever comes to consult her". Regarding the incorporation process,[22] Morgana says: "I only feel when she first takes over me and, later, when she leaves me. Beforehand, no matter how many problems I might have, no matter how full my head might be, I empty out my head so that I can give myself over to her".

Anyone who witnesses a *travesti* embodying a *pomba-gira* will undoubtedly experience a sensual performance that is striking for the aesthetic beauty of the dances, the clothes, the syncopated rhythms, the sensuality and plasticity of the movements, and the mixture of pleasure, danger, and joy. The medium's entrance into a trance state is also marked by laughter and by increasingly lascivious movements, increasingly impudent glances, and increasingly obscene language

---

[22] Trance or possession, considered central to Afro-Brazilian religions, are ritual phenomena that allow people to become closer to *orixás* and other entities. During possession, an *orixá* or *exu* "descends" and carries out performances through a conjuncture of gestures and dances carried out to ritual drumming. For more on this and other related themes, see: Birman (2005); Goldman (1984; 1985; 2005); Halloy (2007); Iriart (1998); Rabelo (2008) and Wafer (1991).

(Capone 2004). Throughout the possession, the *pomba-gira* controls the medium's body: *travestis* give themselves up to practices and forms of logic that they themselves do not completely dominate. Pai Fernando emphasizes the beauty of "delivering [oneself] to *exu*, to the *pomba-gira*". He describes how, while incorporating during an Quimbanda session, a *pomba-gira* takes over a medium's body, and the vibration passes through the legs, eventually spreading through the entire body. "*Exu* is movement; a *pomba-gira* is joy", he says. In this movement and the vibration, the "body is delivered" to the *pomba-gira*. To Pai Fernando, what *pomba-giras* bring to saint's houses "is movement, protection, and within the line of exu". The delivery of the body is what appears to make the strongest impression on him. Here, there is an absorbing circulation between possession and the transformation of a body.

In Portuguese, the verb *incorporar* means to integrate, to insert, to join, to group together with, to link, to associate with, to incarnate, to physicalize, to materialize, to construct, to build. Yet to consider the constructions of *travestis* in Quimbanda, we must bear in mind the subtle differences between "giving physical form to" and "giving one's body over to". The English word *embodiment* has, among its meanings, incorporation, personification, materialization; it has been translated into Portuguese through a variety of words, including *incorporação*, *coporiedade*, and *corporalidade* (very roughly, "incorporation", "body-ness", "corporality"). The Brazilian anthropologist Viveiros de Castro (1996) proposes using the neologism *encorporar* to translate the English *embody*, as he believes that the Portuguese words *encarnar* and *incorporar* are inadequate. This concern with translation is similar to that which I have encountered here in trying to denominate the events in which my subjects participate. In considering '*travestis*' experiences and the unsteady ground between "making the body" and "delivering the body", it might be interesting[23] to use *embody/encorporar* in the sense of materialize, constructing, building, and engendering (that is, bringing into existence) the body[24] and incorporate/*incorporar* in its accepted attribution in Brazilian Afro-indigenous religions; in other words, in terms of the specific "incorporation" of an *orixá* or *exu*.

As we have seen, to incorporate (*incorporar*) means to receive an entity; it indicates an action of "delivering the body" to an *orixá* or *exu*. *Embody*, on the other hand, carries the meaning of acting out or performing a body. *Travestis'* bodies have permeable borders, with certain movements taking place in the flesh and others beyond the skin, in an intense interaction between people, objects, beings, and forms of knowledge. These interactions produce bodies that incorporate elements such as silicone and hormones, as well as different forms and techniques of acting. In *terreiros,* these same bodies incorporate *pomba-giras*: having been (and still being) laboriously constructed, these bodies are delivered.

---

[23] Initially, and only in order to add nuance to certain aspects of the processes of inventing bodies. I will return to this question later in the text.

[24] In spite of the variety of the uses of the term *embody* (such as, for example, in phenomenological approaches), I am thinking here of science studies, feminism, and queer theory. See Mol and Law (2004).

A *travesti* embodies; that is, she seeks to modify herself physically, through *dispositifs*, instruments, technologies, implants, and medicines that change her body. She works with her body so as to make it *other*. At the same time, a *travesti* who incorporates a *pomba-gira* opens herself, once again, to alterity, "delivering" the body that she has so painstakingly constructed. Faced with this new alterity, through the incorporation of spiritual entities, she takes on (or takes in) this other that reconfigures bodies and beings into new ontologies. Perhaps, through these movements, *travestis* are insisting that the way out exists through this infinite construct that presupposes an opening to the Other, in an intensive becoming. A becoming-body, as taught Deleuze and Parnet (1977, p.7) is not a body that imitates, that make itself like, or that conforms; this renders useless the question "becoming *what*?". To the extent that anyone turns into what they become, what they are becoming changes as much as they do themselves.[25]

Understood in this way, the corporal transformations of *travestis* are not solely individual searches; it is also worth insisting that they constitute an opening toward Others. Far from being a grouping of individuals swamped in their particular desires, *travestis*, and their corporal experiences and formulations, appear to tell us that there is no means of controlling the body between *embodying* and incorporating. After all, bodies are successive and insistently affected by instances, spiritual entities, and *dispositifs*; they arise as new ontologies, new forms of being in the world, new forms of participation.

Thus, *travestis* who work exhaustively on their bodies, who are affected and worked over by *bombadeiras*, silicone, doctors, and hormones, who have spent hours learning, who have sought out health services, who have suffered violence in places where they ought to be cared for, "deliver" their bodies to Quimbanda sessions. In both *embodiment* and incorporation, *travestis* make and perform their bodies. Actions, substances, and entities produce bodies.

By dedicating themselves to transforming their bodies, often since childhood or adolescence, *travestis* make themselves Others in accordance with what they imagine. In *terreiros*, their other-bodies are delivered to *pomba-giras*. In incorporating these *pomba-giras*, they bring themselves closer to the alterity that they have always constructed. Incorporation appears to indicate that all bodies always need actions and forms of engendering. All bodies constitute themselves in a continuous becoming-other that rehearses movements of *embodiment* and incorporation. These very intimate movements interweave themselves to such an extent that *embodiment* and incorporation reveal themselves as two facets of the same process: namely, the invention of bodies.

---

[25] Here, I alter Deleuze's phrasing so as to remove the universality of masculine words. In French, the original text reads: "Car à mesure que quelqu'un devient, ce qu'il devient change autant que lui-méme" (Deleuze and Parnet 1977, p. 7).

Poetics

These stories indicate that the entanglements (and untangling) that exist between people, entities (both human and non-human), *orixás*, and *pomba-giras* cannot be forgotten if we aim to bring ourselves closer to *travestis'* own experiences, and to consider the constructions that they themselves judge to be relevant. It seems, then, that in order to take such stories seriously, simply restricting our discourse to negotiations with biomedicine and drugs obliterates forms of action and of engendering bodies that are both affected and effected by other entities and other beings, moved by affects and affectations. At the very least, that is what I have understood from the *travestis* who appear in *Bombadeira* and with whom I have come into contact in my own research. In this case, theory functions in a way that obliterates the creativity (in other words, the creative capacity) of *travestis*, removing the potential of their own inventions.[26] I hope that accompanying their physical experiences, their philosophy, and the potency of their "inventions" might lead not to the posture of applying theories and concepts that construct *travestis* as examples (or counterexamples) of previous theories, but rather to a search toward approximating othertheories and other poetics of bodies.

The term "invention", which I have already used in certain parts of this chapter, might be appropriate for considering *travestis'* own constructions of their bodies, given that it is more closely linked to art than to science and, therefore, is more closely associated with *travestis'* own poetics. Following Wagner (1990), I aim to valorize their creative potential without usurping either their creativity or their right to create. In this sense, this "invention" is close to Deleuze and Guattari's usage (1991), in which philosophy is the art of inventing concepts.[27] Invention is not an imposition of an external form to an inert material, nor is it the fabrication of pure novelty, or the fabrication of a final product from a given raw material. Instead, invention is of the order of continuous metamorphosis, of the world, and of beings constantly created and recreated through something preexistent which, as I have already noted, is itself the movement in which *travestis embody* and incorporate.

Poetics produces an "estranging effect" (Jakobson 1960; Langdon 1999): something changes when we become aware of the poetic dimensions of language and of life. Here, of course, I do not understand "poetics" simply as a question of language or of performances, but of a total poetics of the processes of inventing bodies. When *travestis* think about biomedicine, they speak of schemes, of "arts" and "abilities" invented through relationships. They describe the transformation of bodies as "beauty pain", and as "designing the body". In all of these forms, the descriptive language they choose is eminently aesthetic – in the strongest sense of the

---

[26]Considering the journeys of theories, on which I have reflected elsewhere (Pereira 2012, 2015), it would be interesting to question what potency exists in talking about subversion and reconfiguration, and, at the same time, in ignoring the creative possibilities of our interlocutors. What, then, would be the limits of a discourse that is enchanted by the subversive transformation of bodies, but that forgets the agency and elaboration of *travestis* themselves?

[27]Here, I follow the formulation set forth by Goldman (2011).

term – which indicates a conjunction between formal elements and the processes of constructing bodies. There is a relationship between materiality and aesthetics, between poetics and substances, drugs, and surgeries; between procedures that involve actions, events, materialities, entities, and other beings.

When Xuca leaves her house, she thinks about her body, considering the format of her thighs, the volume of her hair, the dimensions and contours of her breasts, the precision of her makeup and its adequacy to her daily activities. She scrutinizes her body with a scrutiny entangled in imprecise limits between desire and possibilities. Xuca is happy that her *pomba-gira* permitted breast implants and other forms of physical transformation, but she wants more. When she leaves for Quimbanda sessions, she examines her clothes, verifying whether they are appropriate for Maria Padilha, as they were in Bagé on the day the aforementioned photograph was taken. Xuca considers everything: colors, styles, and accessories. Once she is "mounted", she knows that her physical postures will be different, even before she incorporates Maria Padilha, and even before she arrives at the saint's house. A continuous action exists between Xuca and her *pomba-gira*, an action that continuously constructs her body.

The term "mounted" (*montada*) is important. In Brazilian Portuguese, to "mount" oneself is to dress as a woman, carrying out a convincing presentation of feminine qualities. (Benedetti 2005; Duque 2011; Vencato 2013), which implies learning corporal techniques (Mauss 1973). There is also a more ample "mounting" that takes place through the use of hormones, silicone, and surgeries that act on the flesh, thereby producing a greater approximation to what is "convincing". "Mounting" oneself as a *pomba-gira* adds to these everyday "mountings"; like them, it ought to convince. But certain *travestis* incorporate *pomba-giras*[28]: here, to incorporate implies, simultaneously, to give physical form to Maria Padilha, to deliver the *embodied* body, to be possessed by (and submitted to) grimaces, modes, fashions, physical postures, and by the manner of constructing oneself in the midst of these "mountings".

Morgana also has a *pomba-gira*. As previously mentioned, she was raised in a "saint's house"; because of this, she speaks of her *pomba-gira* in the past tense. Her personal history involved a series of consultations, readings, and discussions before she was able to "mount" herself, before she was able to transform her body, with the approval of everyone in her "saint's house", including the *orixás* and *exus*, but especially with the approval of the *pomba-gira*. This is the reason that she never fails to "carry out my annual obligation to [my] *pomba-gira*". This obligation is a part of her life; maintaining her body as she wishes it to be depends on satisfying this obligation. This may be why Morgana emphasizes, beautifully, that "the *pomba-gira* invents me differently every day". Thus, incorporations (and their associated poetics) also operate in and on the flesh. Here, I return to my provisional distinction between *embody* and incorporate. "Mountings" demonstrate themselves to be two attributes of the same process; in fact, to incorporate is to *embody*.

---

[28] Over the course of my research, I came across two important phrases: "mount the saint" and "make/do the saint". For more on this theme, see Sansi (2009).

When they are "mounted" as *pomba-giras* in *terreiros*, *travestis* show themselves to be anxious for a new language that offers them conditions to be seen through other lenses and at different angles, for spaces in which their bodies can be perceived as beautiful and their desires as legitimate. They seek to "deliver" their bodies. These bodies design an intimate relationship between performing, "mounting," and delivering themselves to *pomba-giras*. There is a poetics in the schemes of *embodiment*, in the relationships between *embodiment*, biomedicine, and the reappropriation of technologies and materials. In the production of beauty within a stylistic economy, poetics must take advantage of metaphors such as "designing" and expressions such as "beauty". All of these relationships design beautiful bodies, modifying their contours and their features between desire and precariousness. It is a poetics of incorporation, of delivering the body, of transforming oneself into the Other after having been transposed. In every case, it is a poetics of a body continually invented and reinvented.

Final Considerations

The above histories and theories tell us that modeling (in other words, acting or performing) bodies is an open question (Mol 1999) that always carries the implied question: where is the body? The inventions of the *travestis* that I have aimed to explore throughout this chapter show that the body cannot transport itself to another place without cost and effort (Mol and Law 2000). No means exists of thinking of these bodies outside of the intricate contexts that produce them; any such attempt would be a kind of violence that would deprive these interlocutors of the inventions and forms of acting that they hold most dear.

Inventions of the body are not the same in all places. The inventions I have examined here present new forms of describing the world, movements through which they signal that – beyond problems of representation – bodies can vary. My own experiences as a researcher and educator, as well as the images and filmic narratives that I have presented, all suggest that *travestis'* processes of inventing their bodies, through both *embodiment* and incorporation, involve multiple agents and mediators, multiple affects and affectations. In *travestis'* bodies, the conjunction of forms of knowledge, techniques, substances, and entities come together in unexpected ways, through spheres that are not equivalent, but that are creatively incorporated (bearing in mind all of the possibilities that "incorporation" suggests, as explored over the course of this text).

Although the definitions that I have utilized throughout this chapter (such as those from Mauss, Butler, Latour, Mol, Haraway) are good to think about, they must not be used to mould or domesticate experiences and bodies that refused to be "boxed in". *Travestis* interpellate concepts such as engendering, performativity, and bio-techno-power, to the extent that processes of incorporation – as seen, for example, in the intimate relationships between *orixás, exus*, and corporal conforming – highlight the complexities of ontological politics and design other possibilities.

These inventions and their associated poetics allow for encounters with other questions and with other worlds (and other bodies).

In facing these inventions, perhaps it makes little sense to ask what a *travesti's* body is, inasmuch as, in this case, the body is something in a constant state of becoming, rather than something that has definitively *become*. Above all, *travestis become* and transform themselves through (re)invented relationships. The invention of the body is the result of a gamut of virtually infinite relationships, as though the body itself, with its limits and its potential, were both movement and transformation. Thus, the body creates a particular poetics, as I have learned with Deleuze, but especially with *travestis* in saint's houses, and with Pai Fernando de Xangô.

References

Alvarenga Pereira, M. (2015). É a dor da beleza: as travestis e suas corajosas estilísticas da existência. In *Anais Fazendo Gênero* (p. 10). Ponta Grossa: Centro de Publicações [da] Universidade Estadual de Ponta Grossa.

Augras, M. (1989), De Yiá Mi a Pomba Gira: transformações e símbolos da libido, In: M. de C. E. Moura, org., *Meu sinal está no teu corpo: eséritos sobre a religião dos orixás*. São Paulo, Edicon/ Edusp, 14–44.

Augras, M. (2001). María Padilla, reina de la magia. *Revista Española de Antropología Americana, 31*, 293–319.

Augras, M. (2009). *Seu Zé. Homenagem ao malandro. Imaginário da magia. Magia do imaginário*. Petrópolis, Rio de Janeiro: Vozes/PUC.

Benedetti, M. R. (2005). *Toda feita: o corpo e o gênero das travestis*. Rio de Janeiro: Garamond.

Birman, P. (1985). Identidade social e homossexualismo no candomblé. *Religião & Sociedade, Rio de Janeiro, 12*(1), 2–21.

Birman, P. (1995). *Fazer estilo criando gêneros: possessão e diferenças de gênero em terreiros de umbanda e candomblé no Rio de Janeiro*. Rio de Janeiro: Relume Dumará.

Birman, P. (2005). Transas e transes: sexo e gênero nos cultos afro brasileiros – um sobrevôo. *Estudos Feministas, 13*(2), 403–414.

Braga, C. G. (2015). O corpo trans* no documentário brasileiro contemporâneo: reflexões sobre política e imagens. *Bagoas, 9*(12), 61–83.

Butler, J. (1990). *Gender trouble: Feminism and the subversion of identity*. New York: Routledge.

Butler, J. (1993). *Bodies that matter*. New York and London: Routledge.

Butler, J. (2004). *Undoing gender*. New York and London: Routledge.

Butler, J. (2005). *Giving an account of oneself*. New York: Fordham University Press.

Butler, J. (2009). *Frames of war: When life is grievable?* London/New York: Verso.

Capone, S. (2004). *A busca da África no candomblé. Tradição e poder no Brasil*. Rio de Janeiro: Pallas/Contra Capa.

Carrara, S., & Vianna, A. (2006). Tá lá o corpo estendido no chão…: A violência letal contra travestis no município do Rio de Janeiro. *Physis: Revista de Saúde Coletiva, Rio de Janeiro, 16*(2), 233–249.

Contins, M. (1983). *O caso da pombagira: Reflexões sobre crime, possessão e imagem feminina*. Rio de Janeiro: Thesis. Museu Nacional.

Contins, M., & Goldman, M. (1984). O caso da pombagira. Religião e violência: uma análise do jogo discursivo entre umbanda e sociedade. *Religião e Sociedade, 11*(1), 103–132.

Deleuze, G., & Guattari, F. (1991). *Qu'est-ce que la philosophie?* Paris: Minuit.

Deleuze, G., & Parnet, C. (1977). *Dialogues*. Paris: Flammarion.

Duque, T. (2011). *Montagens e desmontagens: desejo, estigma e vergonha entre travestis adolescentes*. São Paulo: Annablume.

Fry, P. (1977). Mediunidade e sexualidade. *Religião e Sociedade, 1*, 105–123.

Fry, P. (1982). Homossexualidade masculina e cultos afro-brasileiros. In: P. Fry, org., *Para inglês ver*. Rio de Janeiro: Zahar, 54–73.

Galindo, D., Pimentel, R., & Vilela, R. (2013). Modos de viver pulsáteis: navegando nas comunidades tans sobre hormônios. *Revista Polis e Psique, 3*(2), 19–42.

García-Becerra, A. (2009). Tacones, siliconas, hormonas y otras críticas al sistema sexo/género. Feminismos y experiencias de transexuales y travestis. *Revista Colombiana de Antropología, 45*(1), 119–146.

Goldman, M. (1984). A possessão e a construção ritual da pessoa no candomblé. Thesis. Universidade Federal do Rio de Janeiro.

Goldman, M. (1985). A construção ritual da pessoa: a possessão no candomblé. *Religião e Sociedade, 12*(1), 22–54.

Goldman, M. (2005). How to learn in an Afro-Brazilian spirit possession religion. Ontology of candomblé. In R. Sarró & D. Berliner (Eds.), *Learning religion. Anthropological approaches* (pp. 103–119). Oxford: Berghahn Books.

Goldman, M. (2011). O fim da antropologia. *Novos Estudos CEBRAP, 89*, 195–211.

Goldman, M. (2015). Quinhentos anos de contato: por uma teoria etnográfica da (contra) mestiçagem. *Mana, 21*(3), 641–659.

Guimarães, P. (2001). O doutor e a pomba-gira: um estudo de caso da relação entre psiquiatria e umbanda. In G. Velho & K. Kuschnir (Eds.),. orgs. *Mediação, Cultura e Política* (pp. 295–316). Rio de Janeiro: Aeroplano.

Halloy, A. (2007). Un anthropologue en transe. Du corps comme outil d'investigation ethnographique. In J. Noret & P. Petit (Eds.), *Corps, performance, religion. Etudes anthropologiques offertes à Philippe Jespers* (pp. 87–115). Paris: Publibook.

Haraway, D. (1991). *Simians, cyborgs, and women: The reinvention of nature*. New York: Routledge.

Hayes, K. (2011). *Holy harlots: Femininity, sexuality and black magic in Brazil*. Berkeley, California: University of California Press.

Iriart, J. (1998). *Les femmes dans le candomblé. Expérience religieuse et idiome de la posession dans la vie des femmes de Cachoeira, Brésil*. PhD. Université de Montreal.

Jakobson, R. (1960). Closing statement: Linguistics and poetics. In R. Jakobson (Ed.), *Style in language* (pp. 350–377). Cambridge, MA: MIT Press.

Langdon, E. J. (1999). A fixação da narrativa: do mito para a poética de literatura oral. *Horizontes Antropológicos, 5*(12), 45–68.

Latour, B. (2004). How to talk about the body? The normative dimension of science studies. *Body and Society, 10*, 205–229.

Leão Teixeira, M.L. (2000). Logorun: identidades sexuais e poder no candomblé. In: C. E.M. de Moura, org., *Candomblé: religião de corpo e alma*. São Paulo: Pallas, 33–52.

Maggie, Y. (1992). *Medo do feitiço: relações entre magia e poder no Brasil*. Rio de Janeiro: Arquivo Nacional.

Mauss, M. (1973). Les techniques du corps. In: M. Mauss, org., *Sociologie et anthropologie*. Paris: PUF, 365–386.

Meyer, M. (1993). *Maria Padilha e toda sua quadrilha: de amante de um rei de Castela a pomba-gira de umbanda*. São Paulo: Duas Cidades.

Mol, A. (1999). Ontological politics: A word and some questions. In: J. Law and J. Hassard., orgs., *Actor network theory and after*. Oxford: Blackwell Publishing. pp.74–89.

Mol, A. (2002). *The body multiple: Ontology in medical practice*. London: Duke University Press.

Mol, A. and Law, J. (2000). *Situating Technoscience: An Inquiry into Spatialities*. [Online]. Available at: http://www.comp.lancs.ac.uk/sociology/papers/Law%2D%2D-Mol%2D%2D-Situating%2D%2D-Technoscience.pdf. Accessed: 14 Nov. 2016.

Mol, A., & Law, J. (2004). Embodied action, enacted bodies: The example of hypoglycaemia. *Body & Society, 10*(2–3), 43–62.

Montero, P. (1986a). A cura mágica na umbanda. *Comunicações do ISER, 5*(20).

Montero, P. (1986b). *Magia e pensamento mágico*. São Paulo: Ática.

Oudshoorn, N. (1994). *Beyond the natural body: An archeology of sex hormones*. London/New York: Routledge.

Peirano, M. (2014). Etnografia não é método. *Horizontes Antropológicos, 20*(42), 377–391.

Pelúcio, L. (2005). Toda quebrada na plástica: corporalidade e construção de gênero entre travestis paulistas. *Campos, 6*(1), 97–112.

Pelúcio, L. (2006). O gênero na carne: sexualidade, corporalidade e pessoa: uma etnografia entre travestis paulistas. In: M. Grossi and E. Schwade., org., *Política e Cotidiano: estudos antropológicos sobre gênero, família e sexualidade*. Florianópolis: ABA, Nova Letra. 189–216.

Pereira, P. P. G. (2004). *O terror e a dádiva*. Goiânia: Cânone.

Pereira, P. P. G. (2008a). Anthropology and human rights: Between silence and voice. *Anthropology and Humanism, 33*(1/2), 38–52.

Pereira, P. P. G. (2008b). Corpo, sexo e subversão: reflexões sobre duas teóricas queer. *Interface: Comunicação, Saúde, Educação, 12*(26), 499–512.

Pereira, P. P. G. (2012). Queer nos trópicos. *Contemporânea: Revista de Sociologia da UFSCar, 2*, 371–394.

Pereira, P. P. G. (2014). *De corpos e travessias: uma antropologia de corpos e afetos*. São Paulo: Annablume.

Pereira, P. P. G. (2015). Queer decolonial: quando as teorias viajam. *Contemporânea: Revista de Sociologia da UFSCar, 5*, 411.

Peres, W.S. (2005). Subjetividade das travestis brasileiras: da vulnerabilidade da estigmatização à construção da cidadania. PhD. Universidade Estadual do Rio de Janeiro.

Prandi, R. (1991). *Os candomblés de São Paulo: a velha magia na metrópole nova*. São Paulo: Hucitec; Edusp.

Prandi, R. (1996). *Pomba-gira dos candomblés e as faces inconfessas do Brasil. Herdeiras do Axé* (pp. 139–164). São Paulo: Hucitec.

Preciado, P. B. (2002). *Manifiesto contra-sexual: prácticas subversivas de identidad sexual*. Madrid: Pensamiento Opera Prima.

Preciado, P. B. (2008). *Testo Yonqui*. Madrid: Espasa.

Preciado, P. B. (2009). La invención del género, o el tecnocordero que devora a los lobos. In *Biopolítica* (pp. 15–42). Buenos Aires: Ají de Pollo.

Rabelo, M. (2008). A possessão como prática: esboço de uma reflexão fenomenológica. *Mana, 14*(1), 87–117.

Sanabria, E. (2013). Hormones et reconfiguration des identités sexuelles au Brésil. *Cliometrica,* (37), 85–103.

Sansi, R. (2009). "Fazer o santo": dom, iniciação e historicidade nas religiões afro-brasileiras. *Análise Social, 44*(1), 139–160.

Santos, M. S. (2008). Sexo, gênero e homossexualidade: o que diz o povo-de-santo paulista? *Horizonte, 6*(12), 145–156.

Santos, A. da S. (2013). O gênero na berlinda: reflexões sobre a presença de travestis e mulheres transexuais nos terreiros de candomblé. In: III Seminário Internacional Enlaçando Sexualidades.

Segato, R. L. (1995). *Santos e daimonis: O politeísmo afro-brasileiro e a tradição arquetipal*. Brasília: UnB.

Souza, M.H.T. (2013). Itinerários terapêuticos das travestis de Santa Maria/RS. PhD, Universidade Federal de São Paulo.

Souza, M. H. T., & Pereira, P. P. G. (2015). Health care: The transvestites of Santa Maria, Rio Grande do Sul, Brazil. *Texto & Contexto Enfermagem, 24*, 146–153.

Souza, M. H. T., et al. (2015). Violência e sofrimento social no itinerário de travestis de Santa Maria, Rio Grande do Sul, Brasil. *Cadernos de Saúde Pública., 31*, 767–776.

Stryker, S. (2015). Prólogo. In P. Galofre & M. Missé (Eds.), *Políticas trans: uma antologia de textos desde los estúdios trans noteramericanos* (pp. 9–18). Barcelona: Egales Editorial.

Vencato, A. P. (2013). *Sapos e princesas: prazer e segredo entre praticantes de crossdressing no Brasil*. São Paulo: Annablume.

Viveiros de Castro, E. (1996). Os pronomes cosmológicos e o perspectivismo ameríndio. *Mana*, 2(2), 115–144.

Wafer, J. (1991). *The Taste of Blood: Spirit Possession in Brazilian Candomblé*. Filadelphia: University of Pennsylvania Press.

Wagner, R. (1990). *The invention of culture*. Chicago: University of Chicago Press.

Chapter 6
Judith Butler and the Pomba-Gira

Judith Butler seeks to reflect on the insidious violence inflicted on bodies and subjectivities framed by the power that organizes social life in fixed, binary terms. This same power establishes categories of that which can enter into the world of the possible; but what is left out? What is excluded? Butler analyzes the excluded figures that mark social life, as well as the epistemological and ontological operations that sustain these figures. Her theoretical movements aim to escape from a petrified viewpoint that removes social subjects from their historicity, diversity, and complexity. She insists on showing the destructive process of frozen and fixed categories. The experiences of dissident bodies show this architecture and these operations of ontological and epistemological violence, but they also indicate the possibilities of rupture and of transformation (Botbol-Baum 2017).

Butler shows the violence behind these processes of exclusion while simultaneously placing these experiences as means of thinking about the world in another way. An opening toward and for the Other permeates her work; namely, for these Others who are excluded from the world of the possible, but who still show their presence. As a result, they demonstrate the incomplete nature of a universality that does not embrace them, the lack of reason of the power that excludes them, and the emptiness of an architecture that denies them. Dissident bodies increase the world of possibilities: this is the poetics that Butler aims to reveal. However, if her proposal is to open toward Others, if what torments her is violence, who, ultimately, is afraid of Judith Butler?

Performances

On October 7, 2017, I was in front of SESC Pompeia, an arts and cultural center in downtown São Paulo, Brazil. It was a tense moment that had been preceded by rumors and attacks across social media. The conditions for violence against Butler

P. P. G. Pereira, *Queer in the Tropics*, SpringerBriefs in Sociology,
https://doi.org/10.1007/978-3-030-15074-7_6

had already been announced. These conditions, in turn, provoked numerous women's, LGBT, Afro-Brazilian, and human rights collectives to mobilize. These groups organized the *Occupy Democracy (Ocupe a Democracia)* vigil in order to guarantee Butler's presence in "The Ends of Democracy," a series of discussions and lectures sponsored by SESC.

Face to face with those who were at SESC to defend Butler were roughly 100 members of groups like *Right [-Wing] São Paulo* and *Tradition, Family, and Property*. The scene could be drawn in the following way: people holding signs; angry shouting against Lula, Brazil's former president; chants in defense of children and families, and against the UN and UNESCO; chants against the legalization of abortion (which remains criminalized in Brazil); signs advocating a return to military dictatorship; a sign with the phrase "Boys are born boys"; yells against the "ideology of gender"; and, finally, people flourishing bibles and crucifixes.

The protest against Butler was so grotesque and simplistic that I was tempted, at first, to simply ascribe it to the realm of the ridiculous, to smile awkwardly at its shameful display. But soon I perceived that these performances highlighted the nuance of many of Brazil's existing conflicts, laying bare certain factors that, in other times and places, are often articulated in more sophisticated or polished terms. These conservative groups' performances aimed to question the rights and social advances that have slowly taken hold since Brazil began the process of re-democratization. As we see now, this process is still fragile, and myriad legal exceptions suggest that we still have significant work ahead of us.

These protests against Butler lead us to think about our ghosts (Butler 2017; Miskolci 2018), which include: a new right wing in Brazil; moral crusades that insist on attacking small advances achieved through long-term struggles; the open persecution and violence against Afro-Brazilian religions; and, finally, the evangelical delegation in Brazil's congress, and its nefarious role in combating human, sexual, and reproductive rights. With their war-like format and their full-on opposition toward progress, these protests seemed to characterize contemporary Brazil: they were performances of intolerance. Finally, the event of the protests against Butler opens the possibility of understanding something of Brazil's situation exactly in terms of the clear contrasts it presents: highlighting the wave of conservatism that threatens to overtake us, laying bare the violence and intolerance of a context that some Brazilian theorists have previously referred to as "cordiality" or "racial democracy".

However, the aforementioned protests presented these conflicts in overly light-and-dark contrasts. If in these conditions we can learn more clearly about some of them by drawing ourselves closer to the social contexts that made these events possible, we will note the enormous quantity of variations in tones that even a well-trained observer might have difficulty differentiating. Therefore, we must be cautious and subtle in our approach, and capable of avoiding temptation.

Temptations

And first temptation might be to link this wave of conservatism to Religion – generalized, with an uppercase "R" – and to do so directly and carelessly. I recall hearing someone say, on the day of the protest outside of SESC, "Those are the evangelicals", to which someone else responded, "I think those are the conservative sectors of the Catholic Church". In fact, as Almeida (2017) points out, the discourses of both Catholic and evangelical religious conservatives highlight the necessity of contesting secular advances in both behavior and values. And anyone who is more or less attuned to our current political scenario will recall these religious people's actions regarding themes like genetic research, abortion, gay marriage, and same-sex adoption. For example, the evangelical delegation in Brazil's congress increasingly orients itself toward the intense regulation of sexual and reproductive behaviors, dissident bodies, genetic research, and same-sex marriage and adoption (Almeida 2017). Legal projects like the so-called "Gay Cure" are clear demonstrations of these regulatory intentions. Meanwhile, violence against Afro-Brazilian religions highlights religious intolerance through the invasion of *terreiros*, the persecution of clergy people, arson in "saints' houses", as well as in the actions of members of neo-Pentecostal churches who invade places of worship to destroy altars and break religious images (Silva 2005; 2007). While I recognize the presence of these sectors and the pressure that they exert against advances in the fields of gender and sexuality – as well as the violence of their protests – I would like to problematize this narrative by exploring possible openings and mediations, as well as the limits of thinking in fixed categories. For those who believe in religion as a form of knowledge (Velho 2010), it may be that, in this dramatic moment through which we are living, a point of view that does not succumb to compartmentalizing into larger categories and valorizing the point of view of our interlocutors could continue to be a valid and strategic position.[1]

I say this because, guided by the *travestis* with whom I have conversed about corporalities and embodiments, I have grown closer to Afro-Brazilian religions. I have been struck both by their corporal constructions and their general approach to life. In some of my previous writings, I have shown how *travestis* construct sophisticated forms of agency to deal with their exclusion from the power that establishes categories of what can and cannot enter into the world of the possible, and that designates their bodies and their subjectivities as being unthinkable (Pereira, 2012; 2014; 2015). For several years, I have accompanied *travestis* from Catholic or evangelical families who have had to negotiate their transformations and options within a shared language, building new forms of communication. Here, obviously, both symbolic and physical violence takes place, which, in the vast majority of cases, puts an end to all coexistence and to any possible communication. Yet other forms

---

[1] Here, I use Otávio Velho's definition of *religion as a form of knowledge* (Velho 2010). In my personal correspondence with Velho, he also alerted me to the dangers of reducing everything to pre-defined categories.

of action also arise and, even though these are the exception, they make spaces of coexistence possible (Pereira 2015).

Accompanying *travestis* and seeing how they insert themselves into Brazil's public health system while following their own itineraries (Souza et al. 2014) taught me something that I was able to share in discussions held at the Nucleus for Studies, Research, Extension, and Assistance of Trans* People at Unifesp (the Federal University of São Paulo). It was a learning experience, an exchange that was both intellectual and affective. And it was this experience that allowed me to meet a female pastor from *Cidade Refúgio* (*Refuge City*), an inclusive evangelical church. She learned about the Nucleus at Unifesp and sought me out; she was interested in supporting the trans* people who frequented her church, but – among other things –she didn't know what their relationship with the healthcare system was like, or what their specific health needs were. In other words, she wanted to grow closer and to relate more fully to the imaginations of bodies and subjectivities that had been designated as being impossible. Soon, she told me the story of *Cidade Refúgio*'s founder.

The church's founder converted to Protestantism in 1995, when she was 21 years old. She travelled throughout Brazil preaching Scripture, which made her a well-known figure. At the time, she declared herself capable of "curing homosexuality". Her "gay cure" and her fervent prayers relating to sexuality led other women in similar situations to ask: which words and actions had led her to this cure?[2] Even as she preached about the cure, however, she fell in love with a woman, and decided to turn her back on her church. A short while later, she was involved in a serious accident that almost killed her. It was then that she had a revelation: she ought to return to preaching and found a church that served as a safe harbor for the LGBT community. This is how *Cidade Refúgio* came into being. At first, the church was a small temple with a congregation of at most 30 worshippers, primarily gay and lesbian evangelicals. Today, it hosts more than a 1000 people for certain weekend services.

Cidade Refúgio is not alone. For example, Marcelo Natividade (Natividade 2010) designed a cartography identifying "inclusive churches" in the Brazilian cities of São Paulo, Rio de Janeiro, Belo Horizonte, Brasília, Salvador, São Luís, Natal, and Fortaleza. Meanwhile, Fátima Weiss de Jesus (Weiss de Jesus 2010) carried out an ethnography of an "inclusive church" in São Paulo, registering different forms of dealing with sexual diversity. In addition to showing how differences in theology and in moral (sexual) conduct arise, Weiss de Jesus signals the rise of an inclusive or gay theology, as well as of a *queer* theology (Althaus-Reid 2005; Althaus-Reid and Isherwood 2007; Musskopf 2004; 2008; 2012).

As previously mentioned, I became aware of the reality of "inclusive churches" and of *Cidade Refúgio*'s story through a pastor who contacted me in order to learn about how to better care for the trans* people who sought out her church. At the time, she told me: "They look for us. They want to know the Word. The want to

---

[2] For a further discussion of homosexuality, gender, and cure in pastoral perspectives, see Natividade (2006).

know if their options will lead them to hell or whether there is salvation. They want to know what the Bible says". On this occasion, I brought up the evangelical delegation in congress, which she criticized in some detail, along with the actions of "false moralists". She also spoke about the pastors who work in communities to mold the faithful (in other words, members of their congregation) without critical thinking.

This article is not the place to analyze this specific story in more detail, but I would like to highlight a few points that arose after this experience:

First, the presence of homosexual people within evangelical churches, even the most conservative among them. This presence is made evident by, among other things, the existence of retreat centers, such as Vale da Benção (*The Valley of Blessing*) and Missão Jocum (*Jocum Mission*) with programs dedicated to "gay cures". It is as though the very possibility of a "gay cure" emphasizes and reiterates the existence of dissident bodies as an imminent phenomenon. In this sense, it is similar to rituals of casting out demons in neo-Pentecostal churches: by making such rituals central to the practice of faith, they put forth an effective religious grammar (Silva 2005; 2007). Thus, as more demons are expelled, more possible demons arise.

Second, this homosexual presence takes place through a process of unspeakable suffering: gay pastors who come out of the closet and see their lives fall apart; lesbian pastors who are expelled from community coexistence; painful treatments that form part of "gay cures"; trans* men and women who are kept away once they begin their physical transitions. The most common term used to describe these situations is "aberration". As the pastor from *Cidade Refúgio* told me: "From 1 min to the next, you transform from a pure, honorable woman of the Word and become an aberration to be cured or eliminated. This causes a lot of pain, a lot of suffering". There is a biblical framework of actions and forms of treatment for people considered to be "aberrations". Evangelical churches have to deal with the difference at the heart of their communities, and this multiplicity generates conflicts. Even in the most conservative churches, dissident bodies and subjectivities present themselves, showing a world that exists far beyond compulsory heterosexuality.

Third, there is a search for and against interpretations of biblical texts. Continuing the investigation of abominations, many evangelicals allude to biblical passages by pointing to "the homosexual act and other depravations". But there are other possible readings that "inclusive churches" aim to put into action, and these readings bear dissident bodies in mind. Intense debates arise regarding these passages that build other possible interpretations. The questions and answers that these discussions provoke show the limits of readings that refuse dissident bodies; or, at the very least, they point toward other, more inclusive possibilities. It is through this process of putting the Word into dispute that theological possibilities for dissident bodies arise.

Fourth, as I have already mentioned, the places of worship of Afro-Brazilian religions are increasingly suffering violence at the hands of evangelical and Catholic groups. For example, on June 26, 2014, a Candomblé *terreiro* in Duque de Caxias, a city in Rio de Janeiro state, was set on fire in an arson attack. In the aftermath, a Lutheran pastor spearheaded a fundraising campaign to rebuild the temple.

The process was mediated by Babalorixá[3] Ivanir dos Santos. During a day of ecumenical worship at the *terreiro*, Kleber Lucas – one of Brazil's most prominent gospel singers, and pastor of a Baptist church – was present. Asked about his presence in a *terreiro*, Lucas responded: "The vast majority of theology that arrived in Brazil is racist and based on segregation".[4] Kleber Lucas's formulation is similar to the observations of Flor do Nascimento (2017), who points to the insufficiency of the legal category of religious intolerance in understanding the context of violence committed against territories and people linked to traditional Afro-Brazilian religions communities. Nascimento shows that, in Brazil, violence against Afro-Brazilian religions is based on exoticization and demonization as well as racism. These religions are primarily made up of Black people and consist of African and indigenous elements; everything that is racially marked continues to be persecuted from multiple angles, including by the state. But actions like those of the Lutheran pastor and the gospel singer and Baptist pastor Kleber Lucas signal and construct new ways of growing closer that – even though they are limited, circumscribed, and partial – are encouraging in the difficult times through which we are living.

Fifth, these interpretations and counter-interpretations mobilize concepts such as redemption, captivity, refuge, and revelation. These are concepts that ought not be looked down on because, as Otávio Velho shows (Velho 2016), when Brazilian peasants speak of being in "captivity", there is a richness of meanings that this term evokes and brings into action, inasmuch as it refers simultaneously to biblical servitude, historical slavery in Brazil, and current labor situations (Velho 1995). The construction of *Cidade Refúgio*, for example, is based on these concepts.

The points that I have emphasized here lead us to view "religion" as a field in dispute, or as a field that consists of disputing perspectives. There are no signs that the current wave of conservatism will dry up, or that these movements of "inclusive churches" might modify the conservative framework. However, new possibilities are certainly insinuating themselves, building new openings and possibilities of mediations. These lead us to think that, in order to grow closer – as Butler teaches us to do – theoretical movements must escape the petrifying viewpoints that remove social subjects from their historicity, diversity, and complexity. This will lead to the thawing of differences between "us" and "them"; after all, as we have seen, all sides are capable of moving (Amaral 2006; Velho 1998).

---

[3] A Babalorixá or "father-of-a-saint" is the central authority figure within a *terreiro*, responsible for leading both religious events and other activities.

[4] This story circulated in a variety of newspapers and blogs. The sentence cited above appeared in the *Curta mais* site: http://www.curtamais.com.br/goiania/exclusivo-pastor-kleber-lucas-rompe-o-silencio-e-fala-pela-primeira-vez-sobre-polemica-visita-a-terreiro-de-candomble. I learned about the story from Otávio Velho.

Poetics

I began this article by asking whether what persists in Butler's work might be her opening toward the Other, inasmuch as she creates theoretical movements that attempt to bring themselves closer to the creative possibilities of their interlocutors. When we read her books, we perceive how profoundly certain people, performances, films, and social movements affect her, to the point where I would risk saying that her writings are almost responses (in the sense of returns, reactions, and affects) to these interpolations. Butler's works insist on affirming that to reify the Other in fixed identities is to reproduce the same epistemological and ontological violence that excludes dissident bodies. In other words, this reification – even when it appears to use terms like "subversion" – operates within the limits of a machine that we ought to abandon. At least that is how Butler affects me, here in the tropics.

Perhaps the path forward is to enchant ourselves with the multiplicity of agents and their inaudible forms of agency, with the creativity of their poetics: tearing apart this reifying machine; avoiding the emulation of movements that wind up imprisoning us all; experiencing other concepts; and experiencing ourselves through other concepts. It means bending our way of thinking, including *bending* Butler's theory when it cannot be applied. Bending has various meanings, including the twisting of spiraling movements, but it can also mean changing the direction of a given force. It implies winding ourselves up (or twisting ourselves) in Butler's theory so as to give it new direction.

In thinking about what provokes this bending, we could ask – even if only in order to stimulate our poetic imagination and the North-South orientation of the affectations of theories – what would Butler's thinking be like if she could experience Afro-Brazilian religions? Imagine if, along with Foucault and Levinas, she also entered into dialogue with *Iansã* and the *Pomba-gira*. Imagine if while she was in São Paulo she had gone to a *terreiro*, a space that articulates a complex mode of life, by taking in spiritualities inherited from African peoples and reconstituting them here in Brazil (Flor do Nascimento 2017). Imagine if Butler incorporated a *Pomba-gira* or received a saint,[5] or if she heard a Baptist pastor singing with Candomblé *ogans*.[6] She would certainly speak of embodiments and corporeities in a different way and in different forms, because the bodies and materialities that most mattered would be other. By growing closer to other forms of knowledge and

---

[5] Marcelo Niel, a psychiatrist and Candomblé practitioner in a Abassá de Babá Okê, a terreiro of the Angola lineage, reminded me of the story of Giselle Cossard Binon, better known as Ominarewa. Binon, of French origin, came to Brazil and visited the saint's house maintained by Joãozinho da Goméia. While there, she began to feel dizzy and wound up fainting, a phenomenon known in Candomblé as "receiving the saint" ("bolar no santo"). That was the beginning of her life in Candomblé. Eventually, she became a respected "mother-of-a-saint" in the Ile Axé Atara Magba saint's house located in Rio de Janeiro's Santa Cruz neighborhood. Her story is examined in further detail in Clarice Peixoto's documentary (Peixoto 2009).

[6] Ritual percussionists in Candomblé and other Afro-Brazilian religions (T.N.)

other subjectivities, being affected by these other-theories and by other practices, Butler would *bend* philosophies of the Global North and add another poetics to the world of the possible.

References

Almeida, R. de. (2017). A onda quebrada: evangélicos e conservadorismo. *Cadernos Pagu*. Campinas, SP, Núcleo de Estudos de Gênero-Pagu/Unicamp, 50, p. e175001.

Althaus-Reid, M. (2005). From the goddess to queer theology: The state we are in now. *Feminist Theology, 13*, 265.

Althaus-Reid, M., & Isherwood, L. (2007). Thinking theology and queer theory. *Feminist Theology, 15*, 302.

Amaral, L. (2006). Otávio, Provocador de Encontros. Numen: revista de estudos e pesquisa da religião, Juiz de Fora, 9(2), pp.81–90.

Botbol-Baum, M. (2017). *Judith Butler: du genre à la non-violence*. Nantes: Les Éditions Nouvelles Céclie Default.

Butler, J. (2017). *O Fantasma do Gênero*. Folha de S. Paulo, 19 Nov 2017. [Online]. Available at: http://www1.folha.uol.com.br/ilustrissima/2017/11/1936103-judith-butler-escreve-sobre-o-fantasma-do-genero-e-o-ataque-sofrido-no-brasil.shtml. Accessed 22 June 2018.

Flor do Nascimento, W. (2017). O fenômeno do racismo religioso: desafios para os povos tradicionais de matrizes africanas. *Revista Eixo, 6*, 51–56.

Miskolci, R. (2018). Dissipando fantasmas: a política do medo da "ideologia de gênero". *Cadernos Pagu*, Campinas, SP, Núcleo de Estudos de Gênero-Pagu/Unicamp, 53.

Musskopf, A.S. (2004). Talar Rosa: Um estudo didático-histórico-sistemático sobre a Ordenação ao Ministério por Homossexuais. Thesis. Escola Superior de Teologia de São Leopoldo, RS.

Musskopf, A.S. (2008). *Via(da)gens teológicas: itinerários para uma teologia Queer no Brasil*. PhD. Escola Superior de Teologia de São Leopoldo, RS.

Musskopf, A. S. (2012). *Uma brecha no armário: propostas para uma Teologia Gay*. São Leopoldo: Escola Superior de Teologia de São Leopoldo, RS.

Natividade, M. T. (2006). Homossexualidade, gênero e cura em perspectivas pastorais evangélicas. *Revista Brasileira de Ciências Sociais, 21*(61), 115–132.

Natividade, M. T. (2010). Uma homossexualidade santificada? Etnografia de uma comunidade inclusiva pentecostal. *Religião e Sociedade, 30*(2), 90–121.

Peixoto, C.E. (2009). Documentário Gisèle Omindarewa. 65 min. [Online]. Available at: http://oriose.blogspot.com/2013/08/documentario-gisele-omindarewa.html#.W2RcxNVKiUk. Accessed 28 June 2018.

Pereira, P. P. G. (2012). Queer nos trópicos. *Contemporânea: Revista de Sociologia da UFSCar, 2*, 371–394.

Pereira, P. P. G. (2014). *De corpos e travessias. Uma antropologia de corpos e afetos*. São Paulo: Annablume.

Pereira, P. P. G. (2015). Queer decolonial: quando as teorias viajam. *Contemporânea: Revista de Sociologia da UFSCar, 5*, 411.

da Silva, V. G. (2005). Concepções religiosas afro-brasileiras e neopentecostais: uma análise simbólica. *Revista USP, 67*, 150–175.

Silva, V.G. da. (2007). Neopentecostalismo e religiões afro-brasileiras: Significados do ataque aos símbolos da herança religiosa africana no Brasil contemporâneo. *Mana*, Rio de Janeiro, PPGAS Museu Nacional, 13(1), pp.207–236.

Souza, M. H. T., et al. (2014). Itinerários terapêuticos de travestis da região central do Rio Grande do Sul, Brasil. *Ciência e Saúde Coletiva, 19*(7), 2277–2286.

Velho, O. (1995). *O cativeiro da Besta-Fera Besta-Fera. Recriação do Mundo*. Rio de Janeiro: Relume Dumará.

Velho, O. (1998). O que a religião pode fazer pelas ciências sociais? *Religião e Sociedade, 19*(1), 9–17.

Velho, O. (2010). A religião é um modo de conhecimento? *Plura, Revista de Estudos de Religião, 1*(1), 3–37.

Velho, O. (2016). O que é pensar desde o Sul. *Sociologia & Antropologia, 6*, 781–795.

Weiss de Jesus, F. (2010). A cruz e o arco-íris: Refletindo sobre gênero e sexualidade a partir de uma 'igreja inclusiva' no Brasil. *Ciencias Sociales y Religión, 12*, 131–146.

Index

CPSIA information can be obtained
at www.ICGtesting.com
Printed in the USA
LVHW050442130723
752245LV00004B/266